The 50CAN Guide to Political Advocacy

This book belongs to:

50CAN

The 50CAN Guide to Political Advocacy

by Jonathan Nikkila

This book is dedicated to the many mentors, friends and colleagues who passed on their own wisdom and experience to me. Like anything in life, there are few new ideas. I view my own expertise as an accumulation from others. I have been blessed to work alongside accomplished and diverse people who come from many different states, backgrounds and political ideologies. I look forward to continuing to grow and learn from each of them.

The 50CAN Guide to Political Advocacy

50CAN: The 50-State Campaign for Achievement Now
1625 K Street NW, Suite 400
Washington D.C. 20006

Author
Jonathan Nikkila

Editor
Ned Stanley

Design & layout
House9 Design

Library of Congress Control Number 2019910552
Paperback ISBN 9 780999 337103

Introduction

1. Preparing for political power

2. Evaluating a candidate

3. Engaging in elections

4. Post-election to-dos

5. Lobbying for lasting change

Conclusion: The 50CAN Community

The promise of politics

Introduction

IN THIS SECTION

The promise of politics

If you want to turn policy ideas into law, then politics is essential.

Since you are reading this, you probably have a public policy idea that you think can make life better for people in your neighborhood, city, state or nation. That is commendable. Our society is driven forward by movements that began as ideas—ideas that started in the mind of someone like you.

While you probably have a lot of confidence your idea will make the world better, it's safe to assume that others may be more skeptical. In order for your idea to be implemented, it must first go through a process to receive scrutiny and approval. That process is politics.

Politics has been a part of human history for thousands of years in some form or another. Because we are a democratic society, the United States uses politics to debate with our fellow citizens and come to an agreement about our laws and public institutions. Being an engaged member of a community means you are willing to join in this debate. By getting political, you join a long and noble tradition of those who came before you who helped uplift the human condition.

Engaging in politics is also practical. Politics is the prism through which elected officials evaluate public policy suggestions and weigh public support. Quite simply, you cannot make policy change if you do not introduce your ideas to the political process.

This book is a continuation of the 50CAN Guide to Building Advocacy Campaigns. While that book introduced a step-by-step process for creating advocacy plans, this edition of the guide will discuss electoral politics. The purpose of this book is to help existing advocacy organizations (or groups of individuals who are organized around a common policy idea) to successfully engage in politics.

Politics is not an exact science. A good advocate learns to evaluate people and scenarios and adapt based on experience. However, the political world does have principles that we can learn from as we seek to find a political strategy that works best for each situation.

This book takes you through several steps of the political advocacy process, including how to start a political organization, how to plan political involvement, and how to effectively support your candidates. You will be given options for political engagement that cost very little. If you have more ambitious plans, you'll learn about options such as independent expenditures that take more time and resources. At the end, we delve into tactics and how-to's for legislative advocacy that will allow you to follow through on your political success.

It is our hope that after reading this guide, you will feel better equipped to move your policy idea from dream to reality.

CHAPTER 1

What is politics?

Politics is how we choose our political leaders and our laws.

If you get your impression of politics from Hollywood movies, you might think that political change only happens when people resort to extremes—either stirring, "drop the mic" speeches or shady dealings with crooked politicians.

In reality, being successful at politics is about smart planning and hard work. Each state and local political system within the United States has its own processes for considering revisions to its laws and choosing the people who will govern. In this way, politics is a creature of the people chosen to lead each political system. To be successful in politics, you must not neglect this human element.

It is important to understand that the people who govern political systems are much more diverse than they might appear at first glance. Even if they do not appear politically diverse, they consist of people with unique personalities and experiences. Even if the political party in power remains the same over time, the path to political success for an issue may change because the people in elected office change. Even though there are steps and standard tactics you can follow, because of the human element, it is not as simple as following a recipe. Your arguments and tactics will impact each elected official differently, and you need to be sensitive to that.

Despite this diversity, most elected officials do have something fundamental in common. Elected officials believe they are serving in office for the right reasons. They have many goals in common with you, though your path to those goals may differ. In instances when these leaders disagree with you, they still believe they are seeking to advance the well-being of the citizens in their school district, city, county, state or nation.

If you want to be successful in politics you must be committed to understanding both the uniqueness and the similarities of the people in your political world. This understanding will shape everything you do.

One key to successfully participating in politics is to understand politicians are real people. Consider the political experiences and political leaders who have shaped your views of politics. Take a moment to think about the beliefs and assumptions that drive the way you approach political leaders in your community.

What are positive associations you have with politics?

What are negative associations you have with politics?

Which political leader—current or historical—has inspired you by the way they engaged in the political process?

If you were to run for office, what would you hope people would say about you?

CHAPTER 2

Electoral politics is how change happens in our world

Political engagement is critical if you want to advance your policy agenda.

Political leadership is about making hard choices. Take a moment to read the question below, and then write down your answer.

When faced with a difficult decision, do you believe an elected official should do what they personally believe is right or should they follow the beliefs of a majority of their voters?

It's a simple question, but you may have found yourself wishing you had more space to write your answer. If you are like most people, your answer will depend on the specific policy issue being debated and the degree of popular support for one side or the other. Sometimes we may find ourselves in the "Do what is right!" camp. And other times we will be holding a sign with the words, "Listen to the people!"

The truth is that the policy making process is complex because these competing principles are in tension with one another. By spending a little time grappling with these tensions, you help get yourself into the mind of an elected official.

When we look at the world from this perspective of competing principles, we may better understand why elected officials squirm, hedge and deflect when we press them on a policy goal. This tension is best resolved through the push and pull of our political process. Therefore, the ultimate goal of engaging in electoral politics is to help your elected officials see your suggested action as both the right thing to do AND something that is aligned with the will of the people.

Use politics to find more elected officials who believe your cause is the right thing to do

Legislative advocacy takes skill, hard work and compelling ideas. But you make your job so much harder if you are not involved in electoral politics. In many cases your issue is doomed before it starts because, for whatever reason, the elected officials who are in office simply do not agree with you. If they ask themselves the question, "Do I believe this is the right thing to do?," too many of them might say, "No."

That is where electoral politics comes into play. By identifying, recruiting and supporting candidates that share your vision, you can help blaze a path to your legislative advocacy success. You will have more elected officials who are willing to support your issue because they believe it is the right thing to do. Even adding just a handful of passionate advocates to an elected body can make an enormous difference.

Use politics to communicate that your cause reflects the will of the people

It is human nature to seek approval and affirmation. This is particularly true when it comes to elections. When elected officials cast votes, the idea of re-election sits in their mind. They process—whether consciously or subconsciously—all the organizations that engage in elections and the opinions of their voters. "What would they think about how I vote on this issue?" This is how our system is intended to work, especially if you subscribe to the "listen to the people" view of the world.

If your cause is not relevant to an elected official's constituents, it hurts your chances for being relevant when the policy idea is being debated and voted on. Elected officials will believe, perhaps rightly so, that if voters do not care that much about it neither should they.

Just the simple step of being part of electoral politics is critical. Whether it is small things such as holding forums and asking candidates to complete questionnaires, or big things such as recruiting and supporting specific candidates in difficult races, it brings you to the forefront of their minds. Even elected officials who do not agree with you may, from time-to-time, err towards compromising with you on the chance you will put less pressure on them in the next election.

This does not guarantee you will win most of the policy votes that matter to you, but it does put you in a much greater position for success.

Now that you know why politics matters, it's time to turn to the all-important question of how best to get involved.

Politics is messy, but that is the way it was intended to be

Unfortunately, political engagement is a line many advocates choose not to cross. They may opt to participate in policy advocacy but consider electoral politics too difficult, controversial or messy.

Our form of government was no accident. While our nation's founders could not have imagined yard signs and online banner ads, they were quite deliberate with their plans. They wanted a democratic system that protected the individual freedoms they fought for in the American Revolution. However, as James Madison explained in the famous Federalist #10, they understood that the political system would have to work with human nature, rather than against it.

In a free society, people would disagree and political "factions" would arise. These factions would form around people who shared things in common, and they would try to use government to benefit their narrow interests. Those were costs that our founders were willing to incur in order to protect freedom, but also ones that they expected and planned for.

In particular, Madison feared a majority faction that would act maliciously towards the minority faction. To mitigate this, Madison and his contemporaries created a democratic republic, a political hybrid, where most policy ideas were not left to the popular vote. Instead, representative leaders were chosen to decide what was best for the nation and to protect the political and economic rights of political minorities.

We can all think of ways we wish our society could improve. The polarization and negative tenor of current American politics is one thing most people agree needs to be changed. However, politics has been divisive for a long time. Madison knew it was part of our human nature and decided elections were an outlet to express disagreements and provide a mutually agreed upon method to solve our disputes.

Preparing for political power

Section 1

IN THIS SECTION

CHAPTER 3

Keeping an eye on the long-term goal

Establishing a long-term policy goal is the first step of any political plan. Remain disciplined so your political engagement is effective and efficient.

This section takes you through the beginning steps of starting a political effort. When crafting a political plan, you must first answer the fundamental question of why you are engaging in the political process. What is the major policy change you are seeking? This long-term policy goal should guide all your political activity.

When engaging in elections, there will be crises grabbing your attention and unexpected political opportunities calling for your time and resources.

Competing goals (like a secondary policy objective) and unforeseen opportunities (like a mid-term retirement of an elected official) will arise. Your challenge is to ensure that any election work you do in response to these developments is still in service of your long-term goal.

There is another downfall of not focusing on long-term goals. Building election plans only around short-term opportunities may send the wrong signals to elected officials. If you pursue a short-term objective without aligning it to your long-term goal, the elected officials may misinterpret it as your top policy priority and believe they have been bold enough. In some cases, officials you support might even disagree with your long-term priority altogether.

It can also be problematic to invest time and money in getting political wins that do not move your long-term agenda forward. So it is important only to focus on a detour such as a special election if it aligns with the long-term mission.

To summarize, when engaging in elections, you must evaluate:

→ What is your long-term policy goal?
→ How many years can you maintain the energy to focus on this goal?

Once you have answered those questions, you have a lens through which you can view all your political decisions.

In the next chapter, we will discuss why it is important to identify which elected officials have influence over your long-term policy goal.

CHAPTER 4

Determining who has the power

Before you engage in politics, you need to take a close look at how the process works to make the changes you want.

Have you ever bought an unassembled toy or piece of furniture? In big letters on the front of the instruction booklet it usually says something along the lines of "read the complete instructions before beginning." Let's face it: most of us ignore those directions and jump right in. As a result, we might invest several hours, get to "step 12," and find we have an extra part or we assembled the entire thing backwards. We have to start all over again. Political engagement in elections and legislative advocacy is no different.

Before attempting to pass a new law and elect new candidates, you must first ask yourself a few things:

- → What political body has the authority to enact my idea (a school board, legislature, city council, etc.)?
- → Are there steps I have to take, such as a committee process?
- → How many people within that political body have to vote in favor?
- → How many people in those positions already support me?

The answers to these questions help you decide where to invest your time, energy and resources. For example, if your proposed law has to go through the House Finance Committee and you do not currently have the votes, it means you have to focus more of your advocacy activity there. Perhaps every step of the process will require equal parts of your attention. Regardless, if you do not consider all these questions at the beginning, then it is like assembling that futon with a blindfold on.

Michael O'Sullivan

Executive Director, GeorgiaCAN

"In Georgia, one of the goals of our organization was to create an environment where high-performing charter schools have the ability to grow and meet the needs of the students they serve. While local school boards implement educational laws on the local level and can approve the opening of charter schools, we knew that the state legislature sets most rules pertaining to education and charter schools in the state.

To change the pieces of the law we were unhappy with, we worked with our coalition partners to identify legislators who agreed with us and had an interest in carrying legislation to address these issues.

In order for a bill to become law in Georgia, it must receive a majority vote of both chambers of the legislature and then be signed by the governor. However, before going forward to a vote, it must pass through a committee process. Typically, this includes passing out of a House Education Subcommittee, followed by the full House Education Committee, followed by the Rules Committee. While the main job of the Education Committee is to evaluate and make changes to the bill, the Rules Committee determines whether or not the bill will go to the floor for a vote.

In Georgia, every bill must pass its originating chamber by a certain time during the session and then will go to the other chamber for consideration following the same committee process. Our charter-school bill started in the House, made its way through the same set of Senate committees and then the floor. Once agreed to by the full Senate, it then went to the governor for his signature.

In analyzing the legislative process, we felt comfortable we had the support of the governor and support in both chambers. However, we determined that the Senate Education Committee would be a challenge, and even if we could get the bill out of committee, the two chambers would have difficulty agreeing. As such, we devoted most of our advocacy engagement to that committee and worked closely with the bill sponsors to ensure the chamber divide was minimized. Ultimately, this strategy worked out in our favor and we successfully passed a bill to remove many of the barriers stifling charter growth in our state."

Chart the path: How did Michael get from start to finish?

What governmental bodies impacted the policy area Michael wanted to change and why?

What was the first step in Michael's process?

What was the order of legislative process he had to go through to enact his policy idea?

1.

2.

3.

4.

5.

6.

What parts of the process did he identify as potential hurdles that required special attention?

Once you have mapped out your own path to policy success, it is time to begin more directly thinking about your electoral plan. In the next chapter we discuss the importance of timing and planning.

TIP

Look a little closer

When evaluating the process you need to navigate in order to get your policy passed, sometimes key elements of the process are not immediately evident. While it makes good sense to consider the makeup of a committee, you may also want to consider how that committee is chosen. Often a committee's members are chosen by higher-ranking elected officials or a committee of elected officials. You may want to include these elected officials in your lobbying and electoral advocacy plans. Encourage them to appoint committee members that support your cause or have the elected officials speak publicly so that committee members know those elected officials share your position.

CHAPTER 5

Planning for success well in advance

There are key parts of electoral engagement that require an early start.

Were you one of those people who crammed for exams and wrote term papers the night before they were due? Sometimes you can get away with that approach in school, but in the world of politics, it almost always ends in failure. There is a reason why candidates declare for a presidential race long before any election is held. Donald Trump and Hillary Clinton made their first official steps towards their 2016 candidacies on March 18, 2015 and April 12, 2015, respectively, approximately one year before any primary elections. What is true for candidates is also true for citizens looking to influence the political process.

As a general rule, if you plan to engage in an election, you should start your planning process at least one year before Election Day. You will add needless pressure and reduce your effectiveness if you wait until the election is imminent to make political plans.

Among the critical components you can address with a good start:

- → Thorough candidate research
- → Recruiting candidates
- → Fundraising
- → Voter education

With limited time, each of these potential advantages becomes a liability:

- → **No thorough candidate research:** You'll have limited information to help you decide which candidates to support and what to tell voters about the candidates.
- → **No recruited candidates:** You'll leave to chance which candidates you have to work with in an election, some of whom may be uncompetitive or not strong enough on your issues.
- → **Late fundraising:** You won't know how much money you will have to spend in an election for planning purposes and might have to drain your bank account while waiting and hoping for donations to come in.

→ **Late start to doing voter education:** You'll miss key windows when voters begin to make decisions about which candidates they will support.

You may be busy, and there may be other tasks in your role or organization that feel like more urgent priorities. However, if you do not prioritize your electoral work, all your other advocacy efforts may be moot from the start. It does not need to eat up most of your time in the early months, but by having at least some early planning meetings where tasks and goals are set out, it will ensure you are ready by Election Day.

So you know you need to start early, but how do you decide what elections to get involved in and how to engage in them? In the next chapter we walk through the steps of a good strategy.

TIP

Balance partisanship

For many good reasons, issue-based organizations often want to take a non-partisan approach to their policy and electoral work. That being said, elections do not happen in a vacuum. There are many external factors out of your control. Most of the political world operates in a "you're with me or you're against me" mentality. Therefore, it is quite hard to navigate this culture in a non-partisan manner.

Elected officials who serve in leadership often have little tolerance for organizations that aid candidates of both parties. Their goal in an election is to build a working political majority where they can implement the major platform of their political party. However, if you "fall in line" and blindly support candidates of one party, that party can often take your issue for granted or you may be pressured to support candidates that do not support you.

This is a tricky problem, and you may at times have to show preference for the candidates from the party currently in power. The best advice is to be upfront about your non-partisan intentions from the very beginning. Demonstrate you can be a trustworthy partner, able to compartmentalize information you receive from either party. Stay true to your principles, even if you are compelled to operate in a more partisan way.

CHAPTER 6

Creating an election plan

Politics is an art, but everyone still needs a plan.

An election plan provides you and your supporters with the blueprint to invest your time and dollars wisely. It's not too hard to develop a plan as long as you follow the right steps.

Step 1: Choose a political objective

There are four different objectives you can pick from when you get involved in electoral politics. They each help you increase support within the political body you are targeting, but they differ in risk and reward.

Be present
Spend a small amount of money per candidate by supporting elected officials through direct contributions. This is the least costly and least risky way to build political clout, but it is also the least likely to have a transformative impact. It mostly reassures your friends that allies are willing to stand alongside them.

Make a statement
Engage in a few key races only. You may want to make a statement by opposing an elected official. Or, you may need to stand by a friend facing a difficult re-election. Your goal is to make a noticeable impact in those big races and demonstrate the grassroots power of your cause by winning on Election Day. It may be moderately expensive but there is usually very little political downside to trying and losing.

Elect champions
Engage in a handful of races in order to elect new champions who will carry your cause at the legislature, school board, city council, etc. You may not dramatically increase the number of votes in the body, but you will have better leadership. Strong, vocal leadership is a key factor in the success of difficult legislation. This strategy can be moderately expensive.

Elect a majority
Engage in a large number of election contests in order to maximize the number of elected officials that support your issue. Your goal is to objectively increase your support through elections by helping enough supporters win so you go from a minority in support to a majority in support. This is the most expensive strategy and provides the greatest opportunity for impact.

To choose an objective, you should weigh certain issues:

→ Consider how far you are from legislative success.
→ Assess the types of people in the elected body you are trying to influence and determine which strategy will get their attention.
→ Consider your budget as each strategy comes with a different price tag.
→ Consider your willingness to take risks.

Once your primary political objective has been chosen, think of the next steps like a funnel, narrowing further and further until you finally select the races you want to engage in.

Step 2: Assess the current political climate

This step is about deciding what the upcoming election will look like. You may need to talk with many different people who have information about the candidates running in the next election. You may need to use contacts in different parts of your state or your area who can tell you whether elected officials remain popular in their districts. Ask about things like whether the elected officials have strong opponents, if they made any political mistakes, whether their district demographics are changing, or if they are just not working as hard as they used to. You should look at previous years' election data and see if you notice any trends. You should look at public polling and concurrent elections to see how political trends are impacting both political parties.

Your research should help you answer these questions:

→ Will there be any retirements? It is often easier to influence a race with no incumbent.
→ Do prevailing political winds benefit or hurt your supporters?
→ Are there specific friends or foes that may have a difficult re-election race?

Step 3: Decide how to navigate the current political climate to advance your long-term agenda

Once you have a rough idea of what could happen in the upcoming election, you can see how it helps or hinders your long-term policy agenda and develop a plan. For example, perhaps you need to increase support in the state Senate and your support in the state House is fairly good. Decide how many legitimately competitive races there will likely be in the Senate and focus your resources there. Ensure the lion's share of your resources goes towards those Senate election contests and much less goes towards the House where you need only maintain your advantage.

Step 4: Determine how much money you have

Sometimes you will find yourself in a circumstance where you have a key race or races where your coalition believes you must be engaged. You do not worry about limited funding. You build the ideal plan for those races and attempt to raise a budget to fully fund it. For most advocacy organizations, especially those starting out, you will have more opportunities than funding. There may be three competitive school board seats or 20 legislative seats, but you can only go so far as your funds will allow. Assess what it will cost per race for you to undertake your strategy.

For example, if you are doing only direct contributions, you should determine what an average-sized contribution is to candidates in your state. If you are following one of the other three strategies, you must determine how much it costs to be "all in" and reach enough voters to influence an election. This amount varies widely by state or by district based on the number of voters and the cost of the market, but do your research and identify a reasonable figure. Then check the math against your total budget with some simple division. You now have your "cut" number—the total number of candidates you can afford to support.

This leads you to the hardest part, which we will tackle in the next section. You must decide which candidates are best aligned with your issue and which candidates have the best opportunity to win with your help. With that information you will make the hard choices about deciding who you can and can't support with your limited resources.

Sample Completed Election Plan

This is an example of what the step-by-step election plan looks like for a hypothetical state-based organization that works to influence policy that comes before a State Legislature and so engages in legislative elections.

Step 1:

Strategy chosen: "Elect a Majority." We have determined that we are still a good number of votes away from achieving our policy objective in the legislature, so it is worth taking the risk in order to try to dramatically increase our number of supporters.

Step 2:

Key takeaways from the political analysis:

→ It is a relatively neutral political climate with neither political party having any advantages.
→ There are a lot of retirements this year, as many as 15 in the state House, but only one in the state Senate.
→ Two of our most vocal opponents in the House are facing difficult reelections and are politically vulnerable.
→ Opponents in the Senate are politically strong, although two of our strongest allies in the Senate are not and will face difficult elections.

Step 3:

We need more votes in both chambers in order to achieve our policy objective, but the Senate does not present opportunities for us to grow our support this cycle. We will direct most of our attention on increasing our political support in the House by focusing on open seats and potential challenges to incumbents. This is only the first election of a six-year strategy, so we will explore opportunities in the Senate in future elections. This year we will limit ourselves to simply defending our two allies in the Senate so we do not go backwards.

Step 4:

In our state, $25,000 is a strong amount for a third-party organization to engage effectively in a House seat, $35,000 in a Senate seat. We have a budget of $225,000. That will allow us to focus on our two Senate friends and six House races.

TIP

Manage expectations

Once you have built the framework for your plan, be careful how freely you discuss it. Obviously, you want to protect your campaign strategy from being viewed by those who may be opposing the candidates you support, but it also goes deeper than that.

One of the keys to being successful in electoral politics is managing expectations. You are often judged more by whether you clear the bar you set for yourself than what others expect from you. A classic example is communicating about your planned budget. Even among allies, this can pose problems. If you claim to want to spend $100,000 in the election, but only end up spending $50,000, you will be judged by what you didn't spend more than what you did. This may not be fair but it is reality. When you feel obligated to tell allies something specific about your plans, err on the lower end of your expectations. Remember, your friends will be much more excited if you can announce that you have exceeded your goals and are positioned to do even more than you expected.

It is also important not to bluster about the potential impact you believe you can have in the election. A number of years ago, there was a prominent interest group that was upset about a vote taken by lawmakers that they believed were their political allies. The group communicated quite publicly that they were targeting each and every one of the offending lawmakers in their next re-election—several dozen in all. When the dust had cleared, several incumbents had been defeated. That is a significant result; it is rare for incumbents to be beaten. However, the group had publicly challenged all of the lawmakers and the vast majority survived. The election was perceived as a defeat of the group even though they accomplished significant victories because they had set the expectations too high.

CHAPTER 7

Starting a political organization, part I

Your political organization has to fit into two legal boxes.

One would think something as important as politics would be easily accessible. However, one of the biggest hurdles to overcome is understanding the thicket of rules, regulations and laws that govern the electoral process.

If you as an individual (or group of individuals) simply want to volunteer or write personal checks to help the candidates you support, then in most cases you are free to do so by following a few simple rules. But it gets complicated pretty quickly when you want to raise and spend money for the purpose of influencing an election. At this point, you have to create an organization.

In order to start a political organization, you will need to hire a lawyer who specializes in election law. There usually are not very many lawyers with this type of expertise in your area. Ask other political organizations you trust who they would recommend. This chapter and the next will provide you with a basic understanding of the underlying legal questions so you can be better informed when working with your attorney.

When you create a political organization, you have to make sure it meets the requirements of two separate types of regulatory agencies: the Internal Revenue Service (IRS) and your local and/or state election regulators. They operate independently of one another, but all have oversight of your activity.

Internal Revenue Service (IRS)

The two most common types of non-profit organizations that the IRS allows to do political activity are 501(c)(4) social welfare organizations and 527 political organizations. 501(c)(3) organizations can in no way benefit political organizations or candidates, and can only be involved in elections on a nonpartisan basis, such as through nonpartisan voter registration, encouraging people to vote or by teaching others on a nonpartisan basis about how to engage in elections. There are two key differences between 501(c)(4) and 527 organizations:

1. **Transparency.** 501(c)(4) donors are not reported to or publicly disclosed by the IRS, but 527 donors are publicy reported by the IRS if they are not reported by a federal, state or local agency.
2. **Purpose.** The IRS intends for 527 organizations to be the primary electoral vehicles. The primary purpose of 501(c)(4) organizations is usually lobbying or other advocacy efforts (including support of or opposition to ballot measures), but they have the ability to use a small portion of funding for support of or opposition to candidates.

Based on your priorities, prospective activities and budget, your lawyer may steer you toward one or the other, or a hybrid approach of both.

The most likely scenario will be that you create both types of non-profit organizations because they are allowed to have a connected relationship. The 501(c)(4) would be set up first and serve as the parent organization primarily to pay for administrative costs attributed to your political work. Your 527 organization will come later and do the balance of the direct engagement in elections.

Local Law

When deciding which type of organization to create, too many people weigh only the IRS rules. Many are drawn to 501(c)(4) organizations because donors like to hear that they will not be publicly disclosed. This, however, is short-sighted since local election entities can require you to disclose your donors even when they are contributing through a 501(c)(4) organization.

Local election regulators couldn't care less what type of organization the IRS says you are. Each state or municipality has its own laws about political organizations, including when to register, and when to report political activity. In most cases, if you have a donor who makes contributions to your organization for the express purpose of engaging in elections, then you should start with the assumption that the contributions will need to be publicly reported to your local election agency.

States and localities have a range of political committees that serve different purposes. It depends on the types of activities you want to conduct and the types of elections you want to impact.

Once your organization is established, it will have two designations. The IRS will designate it as one type of organization and your local election entity will describe it as another. Both have their own set of rules and you will need to follow both.

There are five types of political committees that you may encounter under local law. The names often vary but the concepts remain the same.

Political Action Committee (PAC)

A PAC's purpose is to endorse and provide financial support for candidates. These committees provide direct or in-kind donations to political candidates. Direct contributions are cash contributions. In-kind contributions are services that a PAC pays for on behalf of the candidate and with the candidate's knowledge. Most states have limitations on the amount of direct and in-kind contributions that can be given and restrictions on the source of funds that may be used. These regulations are called campaign contribution limits. In some states, traditional PACs may also do unlimited independent expenditures, which means they spend money on behalf of a candidate without that candidate's knowledge.

Independent Expenditure Committee
These committees are used to receive and spend dollars in support or opposition of a candidate, but without the knowledge of any affected candidates. This allows the committees to not run afoul of campaign contribution limits or most source restrictions. These types of organizations are common in states where there are caps on how much a PAC can donate to a candidate or how much a donor can donate to a traditional PAC, or restrictions on the use of corporate or union funds. Donations to and expenditures from a committee exclusively focused on independent expenditures cannot be capped, per the Citizens United v. FEC ruling by the U.S. Supreme Court.

Issue Advocacy Committee
In some cases, organizations may engage in an election but do so by not explicitly directing voters to vote for or against a candidate. They may bring up issues a candidate supports and thank the candidate or instruct citizens to contact the candidate. These committees may or may not be regulated by a local elections agency. A few states call these entities "electioneering" committees. In some cases, operating through issue advocacy allows these organizations to avoid having to report their expenditures or donors. These entities are less common now because of the U.S. Supreme Court decision in Citizens United v. FEC, which lifted the cap on donations to independent expenditure committees. It is much simpler to operate an independent expenditure committee and so groups tend to lean that way.

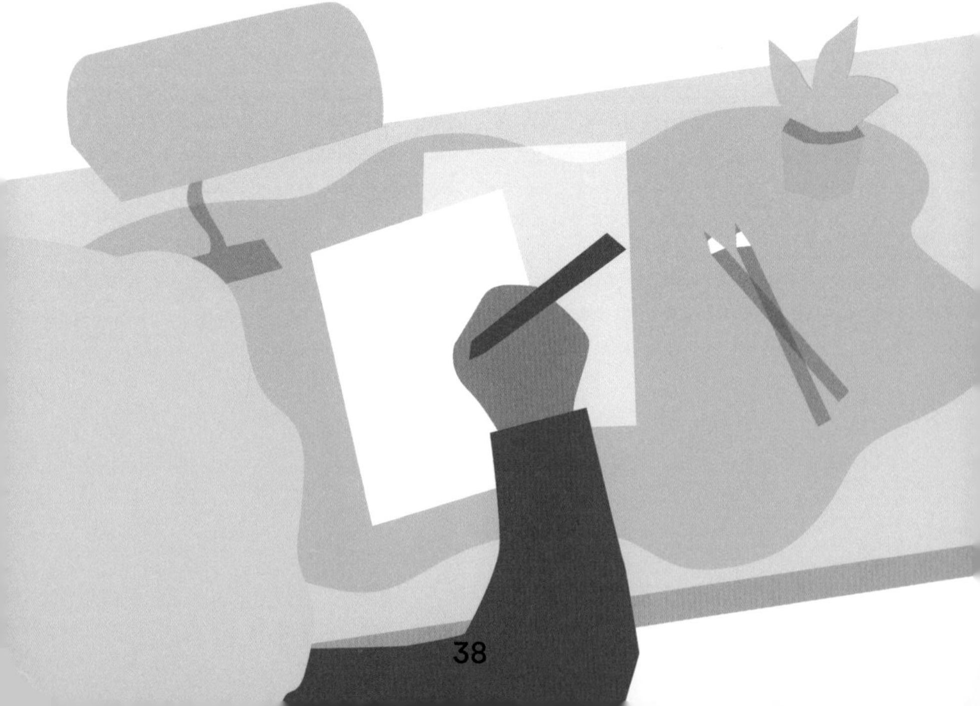

Contribution Bundling Committee
A few states have a mechanism to help individuals make donations to candidates as a group of concerned citizens. Essentially, an individual makes a donation to a bundling committee, but legally the money remains in that individual's name. Then, when the bundling committee wants to support a particular candidate, it gets the approval of each individual to have a portion of their money directed to that candidate. The candidate reports the donations as coming from the individuals. These committees are mostly located in states where there are very low contribution limits from an individual donor or a PAC to a candidate. It allows like-minded individuals to give to a candidate all at once and demonstrate the impact of their cause. In other states, the practice of "bundling"—giving candidates checks from many individuals at one time—can be done legally without the additional bureaucracy of creating a bundling committee. In a few states, this practice is regulated or banned, such as in North Carolina, where lobbyists may not facilitate bundling.

Referendum Committee
Some states have a process for creating committees intended to influence specific initiatives and referenda on the ballot. They are often "one-time use," meaning they are closed after the specific election they are trying to influence is over. Initiatives and referenda are just more democratic ways of enacting laws, and influencing the passage of laws amounts to lobbying. Under Supreme Court rulings, these committees don't have contribution limits or source restrictions. Note that organizations that are primarily organized to affect ballot measures should organize as a 501(c)(4) organization, not a 527 organization.

CHAPTER 8

Starting a political organization, part II

Do not neglect the legal and financial rules involved with running an organization.

Once you have navigated the IRS and state and local regulatory questions about the type of organization you need, the rules of managing a political organization are similar to many other types of nonprofits. You have to follow the law and carefully keep track of where your money comes from and how you spend it. Many effective political organizations have been derailed because they neglected these important details.

Election laws are highly variable from state to state, and they are often fraught with interpretations that make compliance difficult for anyone. That is why hiring an experienced campaign finance attorney is strongly advised.

If you cannot afford an attorney, make time very early in your process before any committee is officially created to speak at length with people at your state election regulatory agency. Ask lots of questions. Restate your understanding to them to be sure you got it right. Talk through scenarios. Take lots of notes, including who you talked with and on what date. Key regulatory questions should be asked and answered before you begin any fundraising or political engagement.

Answering these questions will help prevent the most common missteps:

- → What actions trigger the timing of when a political organization needs to be registered?
- → Do you need the organization registered before you can begin accepting donations or supporting candidates?
- → What does your organization need to report publicly and how often?
- → Are there special reporting rules that apply when Election Day draws closer?
- → How do you go about reporting the information?
- → Who can donate to my organization?
- → What things can my organization spend money on and what types of spending are not allowed?
- → Are there other filing requirements that need to be tracked (corporate filings; payroll filings; business or tax filings)?

In order to comply with these regulatory questions you need to keep good financial records. Identify a treasurer who handles details well. Election regulators are strict about a clear accounting of every cent. Not only do you need good records so you can easily and accurately file campaign finance reports, but elections can get hectic towards the end. It is easy to lose track of how much money you have to spend with everything that is happening. It is important to spend money as an organization only when you have identified precisely what the item will cost and how it will be paid for. If you are not careful, you can overextend yourself and be left without the ability to pay a vendor.

Strategic mistakes happen in political work and can often be overcome. Legal mistakes are more serious and may come with significant financial and political penalties that irreparably harm you and your organization.

TIP

Division of labor is essential

In a political organization it is ideal to have two people with separate roles in the final approval of election expenditures. One person should be focused on the political impact of your spending. They assess whether the organization is spending money effectively. The second person should focus on legal and financial compliance. They are the main point of contact with the election law attorney so that nothing is lost in translation. This person considers questions such as: Are there enough funds to cover this expenditure? Does this spending pass legal muster? Will it trigger any campaign finance reporting? The legal and financial compliance can get complicated and you are better protected by making it the top priority of at least one person on your team.

It is also a good idea to make sure that bank records and credit card statements are reviewed by at least two different people. Unfortunately, fraud and embezzlement are increasingly common in the political world.

CHAPTER 9

Raising funds

There are four key reasons why political fundraising can be more difficult than most non-profit fundraising.

At first glance, it may seem like political fundraising is no different than other types of non-profit fundraising. You have to explain your objective clearly. You have to present a clear plan for how money will be used. You'll need to develop your list of fundraising targets through the hard work of building personal relationships and by paying close attention to who gives to related causes.

However, there are a few wrinkles that make political fundraising one of the hardest types of non-profit fundraising:

1. **Lack of tax benefits.** Donors don't benefit from a tax break and that may limit how much they are willing to contribute.
2. **Public disclosure requirements.** Many donors prefer a low profile and are used to being anonymous when making contributions.
3. **Risk of controversy.** Most charitable giving reflects well on the philanthropist but political giving is often contentious and comes with potential negative blowback.
4. **A wide variety of other options.** Why would a donor give through your political committee to support candidates when they could just interact directly with those candidates? You have to persuade donors that pooling their money with other donors in a single political organization is more effective.

To overcome these challenges, you will need to demonstrate your dependability and surround yourself with validators who are seen as credible in the eyes of the donor. Your aim is to persuade your donors that the goal is of great importance and worth the risk of controversy and public identification. Consider these steps:

→ First, talk about why political giving done through a unified organization can make a bigger impact on winning elections and persuading elected officials. You can more easily coordinate political spending to show elected officials just how strong the support is for your cause. Elected officials may not realize this if your supporters get behind them through a smattering of individual contributions.

→ Next, explain why giving to a political organization like yours may be the best option for donors to help favored candidates win. Not all candidates are made equally. A third-party organization spending on the candidate's behalf may be more effective for persuading voters. Additionally, campaign finance laws often make it hard to support candidates directly. Third-party organizations are often a necessary part of the process to win elections.

Even when you are equipped with the best arguments to overcome the concerns of donors, assume it will be hard to raise political funds. Think like a baseball player and know that even those at the top of their game are lucky to bat .300 with their requests. That means you need to get out there and ask a number of different people. In the end, a good plan and hard work is a great start to persuading donors so they will feel comfortable giving you their dollars and trust.

In the next chapter, we move from the planning stages to the practical aspects of how to evaluate candidates.

TIP

Find leaders first

Because of the impediments that you face in political fundraising, your most effective messenger for fundraising is someone who is donating personally to your political effort. Consider focusing first on identifying an individual who wants to donate and serve in a leadership capacity with your political organization. Their story and their ability to say, "I care so much about this that I gave my own money" will be more persuasive to their peers.

Evaluating a candidate

Section 2

IN THIS SECTION

CHAPTER 10

Evaluating a candidate on the issues

Follow three steps to determine if a candidate will stand with you.

Smart political decisions begin with a precise system for evaluating candidates. Before you provide political support to candidates, you have to determine which candidates should receive your support. You have limited dollars, so you will have to make difficult choices.

The first and most important step in deciding whether to support a candidate is to determine their level of support for your issue. There are three steps you can take to gather this information:

1. **Send the candidate a questionnaire**
2. **Conduct an interview with the candidate**
3. **Use external sources to corroborate the candidate's views and values**

1. Send the candidate a questionnaire

Distributing candidate questionnaires is a good practice for any political organization. It is good to have a written record of where candidates stand on the issues so candidates can be held accountable and so that your supporters, who may not meet any of the candidates personally, can understand why you chose to support certain candidates. It also serves as an educational tool. The questionnaire can include information about your issue. In many cases, this outreach is a candidate's first introduction to your cause and a great way to start the process of educating elected officials.

It's important to know that candidates by nature do not like questionnaires. They take time to complete and put candidates on the spot. Candidates also fear that something they answer on the questionnaire will be used later by you or someone else to play "gotcha" politics. It is common for candidates to pass on completing questionnaires for organizations that they know are likely to oppose them.

The burden is on you to persuade candidates that it is in their interest to complete your questionnaire. Make the questionnaire straightforward and easy to complete. Keep it concisely focused on the most important issues for your organization. You want your priorities to be clear. Write the questions clearly and be succinct. "Yes" and "no" questions are recommended for your most important questions, but provide a few opportunities for candidates to write lengthier answers as many like to provide greater depth about their political views.

Before distributing your questionnaire, you can also meet with other people who interact with candidates, such as political party leaders and political consultants, to build the case for your work. Introduce your organization and its priorities. Help them see that you are an honest broker. Candidates rely on these individuals for advice so building relationships with them helps to build relationships with candidates. Do not be offended if you struggle with this in your first election cycle; it may take time for candidates to see that you play fair.

Some incumbents might argue that they do not need to fill out a questionnaire because they have a voting record. It is up to your organization to decide if a past voting record gives you enough information. However, it is recommended that you send questionnaires to incumbents to ask about their future plans (rather than their previous voting behavior) and ensure they are aligned with your long-term vision.

Some groups publicly release all completed candidate questionnaires and some do not. That decision is up to your organization. Candidates are often more willing to complete your questionnaire if they know it will not be put on the internet. However, if you have a large grassroots base, informing them about candidate positions is a key part of the way you engage in elections.

Ultimately, the main reason a candidate will complete your questionnaire is if they view you as a potential supporter of their campaign. Assuming it is your intention to engage in campaigns, make that intention clear whenever you are introducing your organization.

2. Conduct an interview with the candidate

Interviews are important because they give you a chance to ask detailed follow-up questions and gauge the level of knowledge and support the candidate has for your issues.

Often a campaign aide may complete a first draft of a candidate questionnaire and make incorrect assumptions about their candidate's beliefs. These mistakes are not always caught before submitting the questionnaire. Also, candidates may fill out questionnaires with answers they think you want to hear as opposed to what they really believe. You can flush out many of these issues in an interview.

Your interviewees will range from candidates who have never heard of your cause to those who know it as well as you. You must be prepared to meet the candidates where they are, whether you are giving them a basic introduction or discussing all the nuances and complexities.

Candidate interviews are also a great way to involve your organization's board and supporters. They feel engaged in your work and more invested in the candidates your organization supports.

It is a strong practice to visit the candidate's home district to conduct the interview, if logistically possible. This not only gives you a better personal feel for the candidate and his or her district, but it is a nice gesture on your part to go to them. It may also make the interview less stressful for the candidate.

Finally, keep the interviews relatively brief. Remember that most candidates are balancing campaigning with personal and career responsibilities. Their time is limited and their number-one goal is to be out in the community winning votes. If you are keeping them too long in an interview that means they are spending less time talking to voters.

3. Use external sources to corroborate the candidate's views and values

Most people want to be liked and to have pleasant relationships. Unfortunately, the pressures of candidacy can take this natural inclination and twist it into something closer to dishonesty. Candidates by definition are in pursuit of approval. Some candidates may be inclined to be more agreeable in person than they actually are on your issue.

That is why even with a completed questionnaire and interview, it is good to corroborate the candidate's views and values through other sources. There are many ways to do this. Ask political allies who interview candidates if a candidate answered their questions similarly. Follow the news and see how a candidate answers similar questions in the media and at candidate forums.

Sometimes your concern is not whether they agree with you but what they will say when put under pressure. If you are worried that a candidate may not be able to withstand pressure on your issue once elected, you may want to arrange a public situation where they as a candidate need to face a question about your issue. Their answer will tell you a lot. A candidate who wavers during an election is unlikely to be any better once elected.

If you see any inconsistencies between what a candidate is saying to you and others, do not hesitate to contact them. Be respectful and remind them that you are both better off if you understand where they stand. The hard feelings between elected officials and campaign supporters over "broken promises" can lead to toxic situations and neither side ends up looking good. Once you have a clear picture of the candidate's views, you may not end up being able to support them in the election. However, having an honest dialogue may allow you to have a better long-term relationship, which is crucial if the candidate is elected.

Once you have issued questionnaires, conducted interviews, and validated your information, you may find a candidate that is a wonderful spokesperson for your cause. While that can be thrilling, hold back your enthusiasm until you have evaluated their viability as a candidate. That is what we will discuss in the next chapter.

Sample questionnaire for an organization engaged in education policy

Name

Address

Email

Candidate committee name

Phone contact

Email contact

Facebook / Website / Twitter / Instagram

Campaign manager contact

What do you think {insert locale} does well in regards to K–12 education?

How does {insert locale} need to improve in regards to K–12 education?

What do you believe are the top issues in education policy, in order of priority?

1.

2.

3.

4.

5.

Other

Do you support increased public funding for K12 education? If yes, how do you propose that the increase is paid for?

Do you believe all public schools—charter and traditional—should receive the same amount of per-pupil and facilities aid?

Do you believe in educational choice, meaning students should be free to attend the school that serves them best? Do you believe that state resources assigned to education should follow students to their chosen schools?

Sample interview questions

- ○ Why did you decide to run for office?
- ○ Have you run for office before?
- ○ How would you sum up your campaign message in 30 seconds or less?
- ○ Why do you feel you will be successful in this campaign?
- ○ What are the top issues for you as a candidate?
- ○ Are you familiar with our cause?
- ○ What about our cause is most compelling to you?
- ○ Are there parts of our cause that you struggle with or where you have questions?
- ○ How is your campaign going?
- ○ Who is helping you with your campaign?
- ○ Have you received any endorsements of note?
- ○ What issues have you found most voters are interested in?
- ○ Have you been able to knock on doors yet? What is your plan in that regard?

CHAPTER 11

Assessing a candidate's electability

It is important to evaluate candidates objectively and determine if you believe they can win.

Every year approximately 40 million Americans fill out brackets for the NCAA Men's and Women's basketball tournaments. Casual fans often use any number of crazy methods to complete their bracket, such as favorite colors or best mascots. Some choose based on emotion. They follow their heart and write in their alma mater all the way to the championship, whether their team is a tournament favorite or just lucky to have made it in.

For those involved in politics, we can occasionally be drawn into our own Cinderella stories and follow our hearts rather than our heads when it comes to evaluating candidates. It is good to be inspired by candidates. That is an important part of what makes a candidate great. However, in most cases, the historical trends and campaign fundamentals will rule the day. If you want to be the best champion for your cause you must be pragmatic. You cannot afford to waste resources on candidates who are unlikely to win.

When evaluating a candidate, walk yourself through the following six questions:

1. How hard is the candidate working, and can they express a coherent message about why voters should select them?

Your candidate interview process can serve a dual purpose. In addition to discussing issues, use that time to determine how good of a candidate they are. This comes down to three traits: hard work, a personal ability to connect with voters, and a clear articulation of a message that appeals to a majority of voters. The first two are intangibles that you do not ask about directly but you get a sense of from your conversation. However, to see if they have a clear message for their campaign, you should put the candidate on the spot and ask them to sum up their campaign in 30 seconds or less.

2. How much money have they raised?

Somewhat early on in an election, candidates will begin reporting to their state or municipal campaign regulatory agency how much money they have raised. This information is important. Money helps a campaign be successful because it fuels their communications efforts. It costs money to print fliers and buy ads.

Money is also a representation of candidate strength. People give to candidates they like. The momentum of a great candidate drives contributions more than contributions drive momentum. Look and see how much a candidate has raised and who they have raised it from. If there are a lot of local donors, that is a good indication of grassroots strength.

3. Do historical trends indicate that someone with their political background can win?

Inspirational candidates can help around the margins in an election, but few overcome large demographic disadvantages. If this is a partisan election, you need to look at past elections to evaluate if your preferred candidate's political party has historical advantages in the district or at least an even chance. If they don't, dig further so you can identify how many independent voters or voters from the other party they would have to sway in order to be successful. The odds may be too great.

In partisan primary elections or non-partisan general elections, you should consider other information like geography, personality and issue positions. Assess how similar candidates have fared in this district in the past. You may believe your candidate can overcome historical election trends. Once in a while you may be right, but you need to ask yourself tough questions before you draw that conclusion too quickly.

4. Is the candidate an incumbent, a challenger to an incumbent, or is the seat "open," meaning there is no incumbent running for re-election?

Election data will bear out that incumbents have an inherent advantage in an election. This should give you more confidence in standing with an incumbent friend in a difficult election and cause you to think twice before you support a challenger. "Open seat" races are much more fluid and an opportunity for you to help propel a candidate to victory.

5. Will you be able to collect or access polling data about the race?

Depending on how much money you are spending in an election, you should consider conducting your own polling or partnering with other allies to pay for it. Polling will help you identify key voter groups, issues of relevance in the campaign, and the strengths and weaknesses of candidates. (This will be discussed in greater detail in Chapter 13.)

6. Do local voters like the candidate?

Just like you corroborate the candidate's views on the issues, you have to corroborate information about electability. Contact people in the district or people with knowledge of the district and find out who key leaders are backing. This can include anyone who follows politics closely in the area, such as political party officials, other elected officials, or local members of your organization. Find out if your candidate has a positive reputation. Find out if they have done something to alienate large segments of the voting population. A lot of what you find out will be anecdotal, but if you step back and look at the totality of the information you may be able to see a trend.

Now comes the part when you assemble all this information and draw a conclusion. You may be disappointed to find out there is not a perfect formula for a winning candidate. We all can think of at least one elected official who we thought was an awful candidate and we all can think of a great candidate who did not win their election. What you need to remember is that no candidate runs a solo race; for every candidate there is an opponent. Elections are not about choosing the ideal person for the job. In most cases, elections are a matter of voters choosing one person over another. To draw your final conclusions about a candidate's electability, take all your information about the candidate you like and compare it to their opponent.

In the next two chapters, we will dig deeper into how you determine electability—candidate research and public polling. These topics will help you collect the right kind of data to guide your decision.

CHAPTER 12

Conducting candidate research

The more you know, the better off you are when evaluating candidates.

This chapter is about digging deeper into something we discussed briefly in the previous chapter: candidate research. What you need to know about a candidate is not always apparent on the surface and not always shared with you freely by a candidate. You should always do independent research on candidates because what you find could impact your political decision-making.

Many political organizations hire researchers who specialize in this work. It is usually affordable to hire an expert and it is often your best option because these researchers know how to access information quickly and efficiently. When planning this part of your work, keep in mind that a researcher may take a month or more to do in-depth candidate research. If you do not have the budget to hire someone, that should not keep you from trying your best. It may take you more time to find sources of information, but the same information that is available to a professional researcher is usually available to you, too.

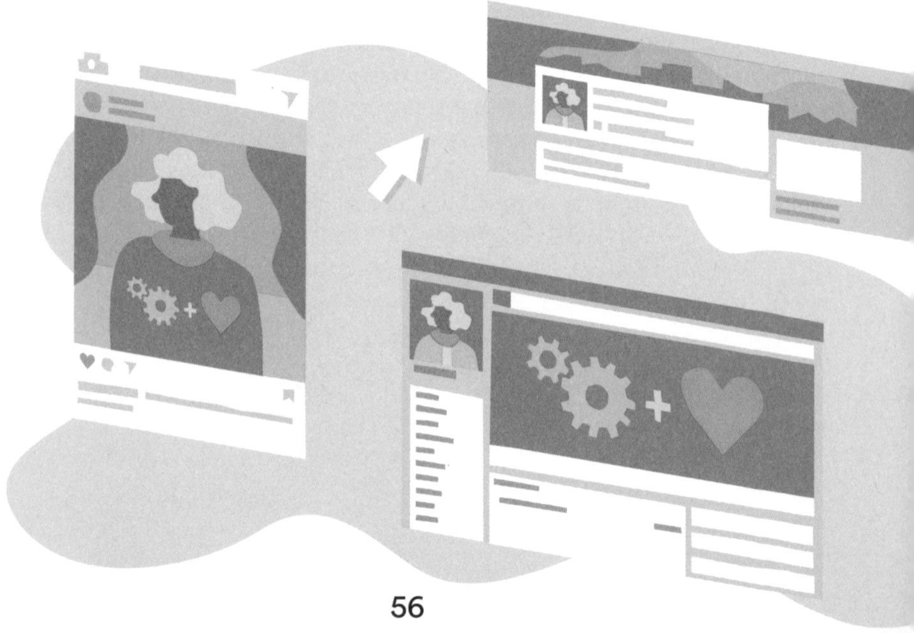

Candidate researchers look for the following items:

- Public statements in the media
- News stories about candidates and their family
- Social media posts
- Legislative voting records
- Personal financial information, such as liens and bankruptcy
- Criminal history
- Voting history

Most of this is accessible through public records or by paying for a basic background check. It helps to have some starting points, such as publications that would have reported on the individual. Talk with people who are following public policy closely and who are knowledgeable about controversial issues the candidate may have voted on while serving in office. That will help you fine-tune your searches.

For candidates you are considering supporting, this information may unearth facts that will weaken their election chances. You do not want to waste resources on a candidate who is doomed to lose once damaging information is released. If you can unearth this information, it's a good bet that your candidate's opponent knows about it as well.

For candidates you are likely to oppose, this information is equally important. Knowing what will likely come out about an opponent during an election can also help you accurately assess your candidate's electoral chances. You may choose to release the information yourself as part of your own electoral work. People can go too far in an election when it comes to speaking negatively about a candidate. However, if you have information about a candidate you feel you would personally like to know before stepping into a voting booth, the chances are good other voters will feel the same way, too. We discuss this further in Chapter 18.

In the next chapter we discuss public polling. Research and polling are closely connected and research should come before polling so that you can ask questions about the research in your poll. You will want to know how voters will respond to the information you have about the candidates. Then, when you are communicating with voters during an election, it is based on proven data and not simply a gut reaction.

CHAPTER 13

Reading and interpreting election polls

Polling is just a snapshot in time of voter opinions, but it provides valuable information.

Public polling, when done well, is the most effective way to evaluate the electability of a candidate. If you envision spending a significant sum to support a candidate, then polling is a wise investment that can also improve the efficacy of the work you do to support the candidate later in the election. If you anticipate your overall spending would be closer to the cost of a poll, then you are better off just using all of your funds to support a candidate.

People often develop the wrong impressions from polling. It is not meant to be a precise prediction of what will happen on Election Day, especially when the poll is conducted several months out. Rather, it is simply a snapshot in time. Voters can change their minds and often do, especially in response to unpredictable events.

A pollster has to make an educated guess about what types of voters will actually show up to vote on Election Day. The pollster asks questions of a "representative sample" of likely voters. If the pollster is off even by a few percentage points (e.g., a higher percentage of Republicans end up voting than the pollster had anticipated), it can change the predicted outcome. For this reason, it is important to closely scrutinize the pollsters you choose to hire. Do not be shy about asking them for references and asking the references how accurate and helpful they found the pollster to be.

You can ask any number of questions on a poll, but the main points you are trying to draw out include:

- → How many people know who your candidate is and who their opponents are?
- → How popular is each candidate?
- → How would the election go if it were held today (called the "ballot test")?
- → What types of voters are undecided and what issues matter to these undecided voters?
- → How will voters respond to specific messages that you think might be used by the candidate you support?

Obviously, it is good if your candidate polls with a large lead, but what should you do when the results are less clear? Here are some key areas to examine closely in polling data.

Negative opinion
Generally it holds that people will not vote for candidates they dislike. If voters view a candidate "unfavorably" as much or nearly as much as they view that candidate "favorably" it does not bode well.

Incumbent strength
If the incumbent is polling well below 50 percent, even with a significant lead over the opponent, it could be an indication that a majority of the electorate is ready for someone new and the opponent may quickly make up ground as the campaign continues.

Voter intensity
The ballot test is often asked in a way that tells you how strongly voters support a candidate, dividing respondents between "strongly" supportive and "leaning." If there are a lot of leaning voters, it may tell you that voters are not yet fully convinced.

Issues and messages
Test statements on various positions for your candidate and see how voters respond. Background information you acquired from your candidate research can be used to craft messages that reflect your candidate's views and their opponent's views. Pay close attention to how voters react to these statements because it could give you an indication of how the race will play out once all the issues are aired.

Party preference
Quite often voters know very little about candidates early in a race but you can ask if they are inclined to vote for a candidate from one political party or another. In a partisan race you can assess how attitudes towards the political parties will impact your candidate.

When you finish reading a poll, you should feel like you can tell a story about the election. You know where the candidates stand at that point in time. You know what the voters care about. You know which candidates align with what the voters believe. You know who the undecided voters are and how many of them your candidate has to persuade in order to win the election.

Remember that the poll is not the election. Leads can shrink, and many candidates will stumble on the campaign trail. However, on balance, by making use of polling and listening to what the polls tell us, you can ensure you make the best political and financial decisions for your cause.

CHAPTER 14

Recruiting candidates

In an ideal world, you want to recruit the perfect candidates for your key races.

Some political organizations may opt to find quality candidates through their own initiative rather than simply evaluating the candidates who have filed for an election. Although it is time consuming, this can lead to greater success if the goal is to see friends of your cause elected. Succeeding in this approach means finding a candidate who supports your cause, will work hard, fits the character of the district and can appeal to voters.

You do not have to be an experienced political operative to recruit a candidate. It is mostly about hard work and being good at reading people. At the same time, this is a long process that will take lots of meetings in coffee shops and around kitchen tables. The first time you do it, choose just one or two key districts that matter most to you.

One legal note to keep in mind is that your election authority may restrict you from being involved with independent expenditures to aid a candidate if you helped to recruit that candidate, even if you have no further involvement in their campaign. Find the answer to this legal question first if you want to have a role in independent expenditures.

Candidate recruitment is not that different than the process of deciding which of the declared candidates to support. The primary difference is that you apply those lessons before a candidate files to run for office as opposed to after.

However, there are a few key differences you must keep in mind:

1. Start even earlier

It may take many phone calls, meetings and failures before you find the candidate you want for a single race, let alone if you are recruiting for multiple races. This process of finding viable options may take months, and prospective candidates may ruminate on the idea longer than you would like. Your likelihood of success is greatly increased if you start this process far ahead of the election filing deadline.

2. Build district connections

Do not imagine you can walk into an area where you have no contacts and no experience and recruit a good candidate. Candidate recruitment takes relationships with people in the district, especially those who know the district. If you do not have connections, lean on allies who do. Once you have the contacts you need, prepare to make phone call after phone call to find that "friend of a friend" who is the perfect fit for the race.

3. Be understanding

Running for political office is a big deal. You are asking a prospective candidate to invest countless hours of their life, which means time away from their family, their other interests and their career. They are putting their name out there for voters and they could be rejected. This frightens some prospective candidates. They likely are not going to be persuaded to take a leap of faith by someone they do not trust. Be understanding of the difficult decision they face. Be honest with them. And most of all, be patient.

4. Manage expectations

While doing your work to persuade a prospective candidate, you want to be careful to manage their expectations. Ultimately, a candidate needs to decide entering an election is the right thing to do because they are personally passionate about it. You need a candidate that is self-motivated and ready to run. Do not promise anything you are not absolutely sure you can deliver. Be realistic about what you can offer them in terms of your time, campaign fundraising or campaign strategy. You want a candidate entering the race with eyes wide open.

Once you have found the candidates you want to support (through your own recruiting or by evaluating the registered candidates), it is time to help propel them to victory. In the next section we move on to what that support actually looks like.

Train candidates on effective campaigning techniques

A great way to recruit good candidates for elected office is to offer campaign training to your grassroots supporters. Many people are interested in running for office but do not know how to start. This training helps you create a bench of strong, future candidates that support your cause. It helps establish your political pedigree with allies, donors and candidates. While it may take time to develop, it is relatively inexpensive.

You can cast a wide net and promote a training event in order to draw people to it, or you can make the event invite-only, bringing together a small group to train.

Schedule the training well in advance of the next election. This ensures that if you do inspire a good potential candidate, they have plenty of time to begin their campaign. Also, some states may consider campaign training as a donation to a candidate's campaign. If you do it early enough and they are not yet an official candidate, then you avoid this complication. If you want to invite current candidates, inquire with your attorney or your local campaign finance regulatory agency. You can also avoid this by having current candidates pay for the training.

Hold the training on a single day. Choose a time, date and location that is most convenient for candidates. If you are in a large state, you may consider holding trainings in multiple locations. Build a curriculum and list of speakers that address areas such as message development, fundraising, communicating with voters and getting out the vote.

Engaging in elections

Section 3

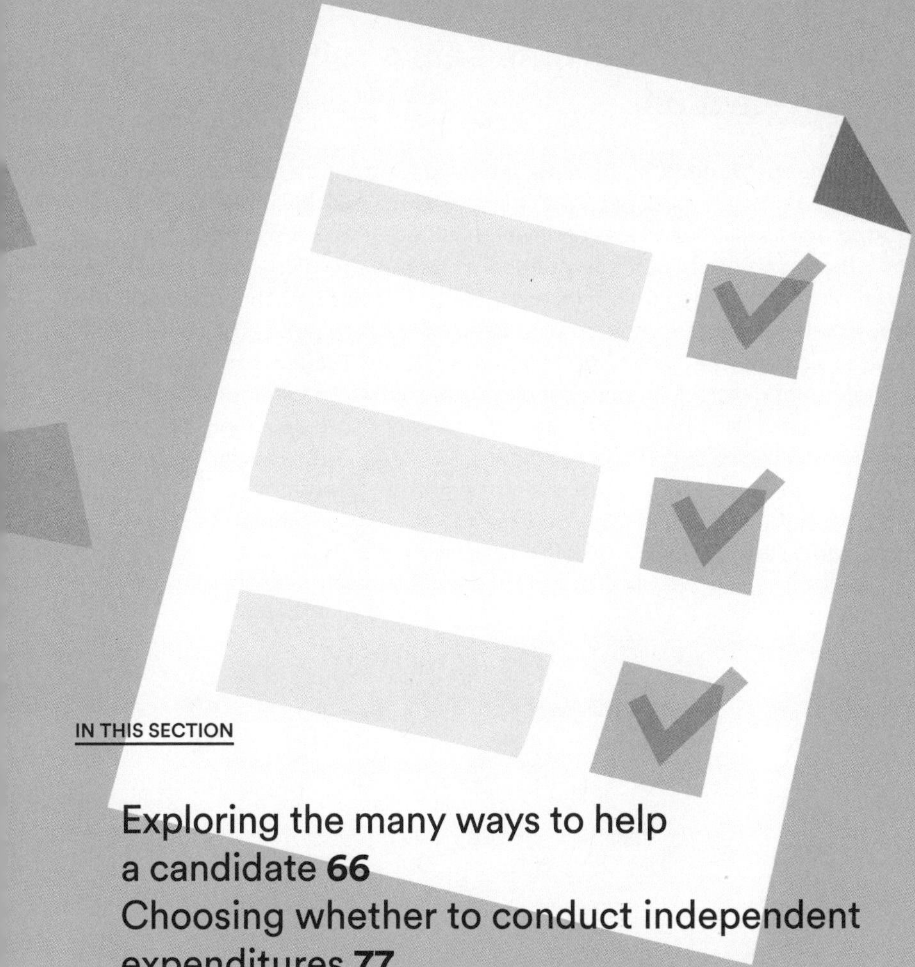

IN THIS SECTION

CHAPTER 15

Exploring the many ways to help a candidate

You have a big toolkit to help a candidate win an election.

You have spent months planning and preparing for an election. You have thought through many hypothetical situations and had to make difficult judgement calls. You are eager to take action. That time is now.

Too many people balk at political engagement because they feel that it is too costly. If they do not have a super-sized budget, then they assume they cannot have an impact. That is a strategic mistake. There are many ways to help a candidate. While some types of engagement require large amounts of money, you can carry out other types of engagement for free.

To begin this section we will list some of the more common considerations when supporting a candidate, including relative cost and impact. Most of the items in this section are best done within a political organization, but some are things that people in your organization can do as individuals with little or no formal support.

Voter Registration

Cost	Lots of time, minimal expenses
Risk	●●○○○
Reward	●○○○○
Timing	1–6 months before election

This is the process of identifying residents in a particular area that are not registered to vote and getting them on the voter rolls.

Your first step would be to acquire legal instructions from your state election commission about registering voters. Then, identify the best avenue or avenues for meeting unregistered voters, such as at public events or in public locations, by going door-to-door or by targeting your existing grassroots supporters.

There is some legal risk in this because states usually have specific rules about how you can and cannot work to register people to vote. However, the rules are usually clear, and as long as you follow those, it is safe.

Realistically, unless you have a massive, intensive voter registration effort over a long period of time or a concentrated population within a target district that you can easily reach, you are unlikely to shift the balance in any election in one year. In addition, voter registration is quite time consuming. It can be a nice public-relations effort or way to engage your grassroots, but its impact will be limited.

Workshops to Train Candidates on Policy Issues

Cost	Modest time and expense
Risk	●○○○○
Reward	●●○○○
Timing	3–7 months before Election Day

Events or workshops where you train candidates on your policy issues are not direct support, but they are a great way to help candidates and your issue. There are several benefits:

→ **Allows you to provide resources to your candidates.** Candidates are often starving for information on issues that will allow them to demonstrate their preparedness to voters. They are looking for opportunities to be educated. You are valuable to them if you can provide this help.

→ **Lets you stay ahead of misleading information.** Candidates are often pushed to make snap-judgments on issues in order to win support from key constituents. That means they may tie themselves to positions and promises that will prevent them from being able to work with you in the future. Providing information about your issue ahead of time ensures candidates have the full picture.

→ **Allows you to promote your cause for free.** If you train a candidate, that person can talk about your issue every day on the campaign trail. You want to give them the right tools to talk about your issue so you can make sure they are making the most effective arguments, for your sake and theirs.

Consider scheduling your events earlier in the election cycle and choose locations that are convenient for candidates. Additionally, think about whether you have strong allies you can invite as a co-sponsor to make the event more attractive to candidates. Keep the program concise, such as half a day, so candidates get good information but do not feel that they have to give up valuable time. Feature speakers who will be entertaining and informative. Invite candidates through multiple avenues, including personal calls.

Endorse Candidates

Cost	Only your time
Risk	●●○○○
Reward	●●○○○
Timing	At any time during a campaign

Some organizations publicly endorse candidates. They do this to draw attention to their cause and because they believe that public knowledge about the endorsement will help the candidates gain support from voters.

Realistically, most organizations overvalue their own clout with voters, but it is possible that your organization's name, issue or public reputation is a valuable signal to voters. Even if there is little impact on voters, candidates often like to build a long list of endorsements to demonstrate their credibility.

Some candidates you support may take the opposite view about a public endorsement and prefer you not make it known or at least prefer you release it at a time they find more convenient. You may want to think twice about supporting a candidate that will not publicly stand by you but as long as their reasons are legitimate it is generally a good idea to respect their wishes.

Campaign Volunteering

Cost	Only your time
Risk	●○○○○
Reward	●●●○○
Timing	At any time during a campaign

Assist a few key candidates in their races by helping them in their voter outreach. Make phone calls or go door-to-door with the candidate once, twice or on a regular basis. Help them stuff envelopes or whatever they need. Candidates appreciate financial support, but they build a strong bond with those who invest personal time volunteering for their campaigns. Do your best to confirm that when you volunteer, you will be doing it directly with the candidate.

If you have a group of good grassroots supporters within your organization, particularly if they live in the district you are targeting, consider bringing them regularly to volunteer as well. The candidate will appreciate this, and it will help them build relationships with your supporters.

You can definitely volunteer for a campaign as an individual on your own time, no matter what type of organization you work for. If you do it on paid time, you should check state campaign finance laws to ensure this does not count as an "in-kind donation." Some states allow people who work for political organizations to volunteer without it counting as a contribution to the candidate's campaign.

Grassroots Candidate Meetings

Cost	Modest time and limited costs
Risk	●○○○○
Reward	●●●○○
Timing	As soon as candidates begin filing, up until two weeks before the election

This is something to consider as an organization if you have at least a modest-sized grassroots contingent. You can also do it as an individual outside of your organization by inviting people you know that live in the district, whether they have engaged with your issue or not.

If you can bring 10 or more people into a private setting with a district-based candidate (legislative, municipal, school board, etc.) the candidate will usually find it valuable. You are helping them get direct access to constituents who are inclined to support the candidate and to become that candidate's supporters and volunteers. Schedule it for an hour, circle some chairs in an intimate setting, such as a living room or small conference room, and have light refreshments.

This is another great way to provide an engagement opportunity for your grassroots supporters. They will likely be enthused and flattered that you are bringing candidates to meet with them and hear from them.

Never discourage your supporters from challenging a candidate and asking tough questions, but in a private setting like this ensure the dialogue is civil and professional. Being "ambushed" in a meeting never sits well with a candidate.

Political Fundraising Events

Cost Modest time and limited costs
Risk ●●○○○
Reward ●●●○○
Timing Best done early or in the middle of the election campaign

A political fundraising event is slightly more risky than a grassroots candidate meeting because you have to check campaign finance issues, but it is double the value to a candidate. You are helping them raise money and connect directly with district voters or other influential actors in politics.

You can hold political fundraising events as part of your organization or as an individual. Set a date that gives you plenty of time to plan and send out invitations. If you pay for the costs of the event, you may need to report the cost to the candidate as an in-kind contribution.

The hard part is recruiting attendees because you are not just asking for their time. Your invitees know there is an expectation that they will donate. Some events ask for specific amounts and other events leave it open to the attendees to decide.

When planning the event, be clear with the candidate what you are delivering. Are you inviting people but are making no guarantees about what people will donate? Is there a specific amount you are trying to raise from attendees?

Find a modest-sized venue that will be intimate but will give your guests elbow room to move around. A private home is a good option and attendees often like that more than a commercial venue. Have light refreshments. Allow ample time for mingling and 15–30 minutes for the candidate to speak briefly and take questions.

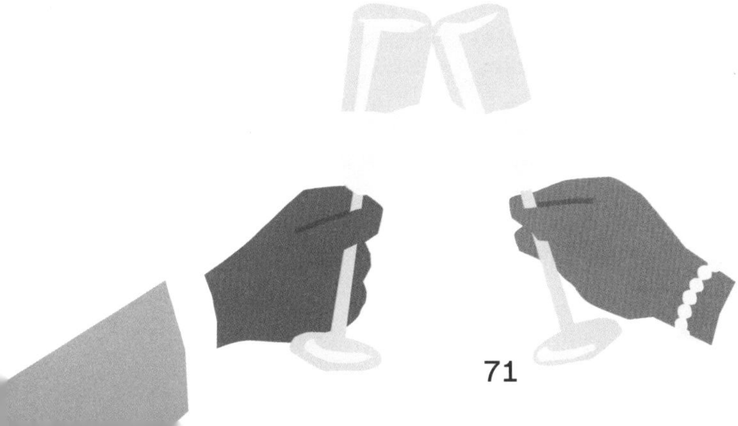

Direct Donation

Cost	Modest time and cost
Risk	●●●○○
Reward	●●●○○
Timing	Candidates need funds before and throughout their campaign.

Direct donations are donations made to a candidate from your political committee or from a group of organized individuals. The candidate is then able to use those funds to pay for campaign expenses. This is the most traditional form of electoral engagement.

The impact of political engagement through donations is limited, since you are only contributing a small percentage of what it takes to run and win an election. Yet, it is a great way to start direct engagement in elections because you do not necessarily need to have a big bank account.

Your fundraising potential determines how many candidates you can support, but there is no minimum. Start with whatever amount you can afford. Once you have a budget, find out what political organizations typically donate to candidates for the type of office you are targeting. You are not compelled to give this amount or to give all candidates the same amount, but it is a good benchmark to know.

There are several groups of candidates you should consider supporting with political giving. There are always exceptions to the rule, but generally you want to give to candidates in this priority order:

→ Purchase tickets for you and other key allies to attend political events and fundraisers.
→ Make donations to key supporters.
→ Donate to candidates in top-priority, competitive election contests.
→ Donate to candidates in races of secondary priority.
→ Donate to a wider group of incumbent elected officials who are part of your coalition.

You will need to have a clear philosophy for who you give to and why. This will help ensure you stay within your budget and so you can explain why you chose to give to one candidate and not another when asked. There will always be candidates who wonder why they were left out.

Whenever possible, hand-deliver contribution checks. It is another opportunity to interact with a candidate. If you have a board for your political committee or have grassroots supporters from the district of a candidate you are supporting, ask them to help deliver the contributions. Generally speaking, it is bad form and sometimes illegal to deliver contribution checks to elected officials at their official offices. If you are not sure, just ask the elected official or their campaign manager for an ideal place to meet.

Canvassing for Candidates

Cost	Significant time and modest cost (dependent on whether you are paying your workers)
Risk	●●●○○
Reward	●●●●○
Timing	Most effective once voters have begun to pay close attention; any time from three months before Election Day to Election Day

Canvassing is usually defined as any personal connection a candidate or their supporters make with a likely voter. Traditionally, this is done by phone or door-to-door. Modern technology has given people the ability to use texting or social media. However, knocking on doors continues to be the best option. In most instances, this represents clear engagement in an election and must be done by a political committee. There will likely be campaign finance reporting implications, but as long as you are well organized, those issues can be managed.

Canvassing is a low-profile but high-impact activity. The advantage is that it usually costs much less than producing a radio ad or a direct-mail piece. The disadvantage is that it takes a lot of organizing prowess and time to execute. You have to make fliers and develop lists of voters to visit. Or, if you do phone calls, you need to find a venue to host workers and get a list of voters that includes phone numbers. If you can become a "pro" at organizing, then you can be quite effective with limited funds. We will talk more about how to acquire lists of voters in Chapter 19.

Door-to-door and phone calls are ways your passionate grassroots supporters can volunteer, but you should consider paying them for their time if possible. A small stipend goes a long way to ensure workers show up. You do not have to enlist only your grassroots. There are many professionals who will do this on your organization's behalf.

In most circumstances, you cannot do this in coordination with a candidate. That is because the cost may exceed the amount you are allowed to donate directly to a candidate. However, sometimes you might prefer working directly with a candidate because it is particularly important that all the election activity is in sync. If your state has high campaign contribution limits to candidates, then the cost of the work may fall under that amount and you can provide it to the candidate as an in-kind contribution. Or, on the other hand, you may be able to help the candidate find volunteers from your ranks of supporters, but you may not be able to provide any financial incentive to the volunteers.

Independent Expenditures

Cost	Modest to high financial costs.
Risk	●●●●○
Reward	●●●●●
Timing	Most effective once voters have begun to pay close attention; any time from three months before Election Day to Election Day

Organizations with the greatest political impact utilize independent expenditures, which involves your organization spending money to communicate directly with voters on behalf of a candidate. Canvassing for candidates is a subset of this activity. Other types of activity could include paid phone calls, direct mailers, online ads, mobile ads, television ads, radio spots, newspaper ads, and billboards. Your goal and your challenge is to determine what type of political activity and what types of messages you can inject into a campaign to help your candidate without duplicating what is already being done.

All of this can be expensive, but like direct donations, the cost of these expenditures vary depending on the cost of elections in your state or locality. You can also manage the cost by choosing only the expenditures that match your budget.

When you decide to engage through independent expenditures, it often triggers rules about whether and how much you can talk with a candidate you are supporting. In general, it is best to have no discussions with a candidate about their election strategy, even prior to independent expenditures being planned, and to stop discussions on any topic once independent expenditures are planned. There may also be rules about how you need to publicly report that your organization paid for the communication, both in the communication itself and through reports filed with campaign finance regulatory agencies. All of this should be discussed with your attorney long before any independent expenditures are produced. In the next chapter, we'll consider the various risks and benefits of making independent expenditures in greater detail.

TIP

When helping a candidate with their election, there is not really such a thing as starting "too early" but you can be too late

Once you have decided to support a candidate, and the candidate is actively campaigning, then there is probably something you can do. The majority of election activity occurs when voters start paying close attention. The conventional wisdom for most state and local elections is that window starts about two or three months before Election Day. For your standard November election, Labor Day is considered the start of the final sprint.

However, support can come too late. If you wait until votes start to come in, you have missed the ability to influence those votes. Not every state does it this way, but many states have moved to early absentee or early voting systems. Many voters are making up their mind and submitting their vote approximately a month before Election Day. If you have not made your donations to candidates or begun doing independent expenditures by that time, it severely limits the impact you can have.

CHAPTER 16

Choosing whether to conduct independent expenditures

Independent expenditures should be the ultimate goal of most political organizations because they give you the greatest ability to influence elections.

Independent expenditures occur when a third-party political organization uses funds to speak directly to voters about candidates, but the organization does so without involving the candidate they are supporting. The third-party groups do this because candidates are often limited in the amount of money they can receive from donations. In states with large or no campaign contribution limits for candidates, third-party groups are less active with independent expenditures. However, in states with contribution limits, third-party groups try to fill in the gaps by doing their own election advertising for a candidate.

Independent expenditures are the most significant way you as a political organization can impact an important political race. No matter which strategy you selected for your political plan in Chapter 6, and no matter how many races you have chosen to target, independent expenditures are the tactic that puts you most in control of reaching your goal.

Independent expenditures allow you to spend an unlimited amount in the race, as opposed to a modest donation. You are able to take advantage of mediums a candidate may not be able to afford, such as radio or television. At the conclusion of a successful race, while a candidate will and should always get the majority of the credit, political observers will note your impact.

There are always exceptions and situations when you may not need to conduct independent expenditures. Another allied group might do a great job with independent expenditures, so you may choose to defer. If the number of voters in an election is small, you might conclude you are better off working directly with your candidate and urging them to spend more time going door-to-door. However, if your goal is impacting larger elections, then independent expenditures are an ideal tool.

What keeps you from choosing independent expenditures has more to do with the success of your fundraising and your willingness to take risks.

Determining the costs is relatively straightforward. Keep in mind that ideally you will pay to communicate with likely voters multiple times over the course of a race. However, depending on the type of voter-contact methods you use, and the number of voters you want to reach, that strategy might be cost prohibitive.

Assessing risk is more complicated to work through. With high reward comes high risk.

First, there are legal issues to navigate. You have to work deliberately to avoid violating your jurisdiction's rules for coordination. Third-party groups that do independent expenditures cannot "coordinate" their expenditures with a candidate or anyone closely connected to that candidate's campaign. "Coordination" can mean different things in different jurisdictions, so you should ask for that definition from your election attorney. If coordination occurs, the expenditure then becomes an "in-kind" donation to a candidate and in most cases this donation would exceed the limit a group can donate to a candidate, leading to a fairly severe campaign finance violation. You can carefully study these regulations to mitigate risk. Hundreds of organizations around the nation do it every election, but it creates headaches.

Secondly, there is the possibility that by directly engaging with voters, you could have a negative influence on a candidate's campaign rather than the positive one you desire. This happens if you insert a political message into the campaign that is not well conceived and backfires with voters. Sometimes voters may object to third-party groups engaging in the election altogether, but that effect is usually overstated. Instead, it is the poor political strategy decisions that third-party groups may make that might lead to objections.

If you choose to accept the challenge and do independent expenditures, the next step is to select the voters you want to communicate with in a particular campaign and choose the messages that resonate with them.

CHAPTER 17

Delivering a clear message to voters

Finding the right issue to inject into an election is tricky, but you can seek support.

When conducting independent expenditures, your central goal is to help your favored candidate win. You win an election by ensuring as many voters as possible know who your candidate is and that they hear key messages, increasing the odds that they will select your candidate in the voting booth.

When creating a message for your independent expenditures, one common option is to choose generic messaging with traditional themes. At this point you are focusing on the public awareness of the candidate and making expenditures that will allow your candidate's name to be seen more frequently. While that is half the battle, you might be missing an opportunity to maximize your effectiveness. The better option is to target specific messages to specific groups of likely voters. This takes more planning and political skill but can be both more effective and more affordable.

Here are the three things you need to know to maximize your messaging:

1. The key to good political messaging is repetition

Any good candidate has a strong but brief statement that drives home their most important campaign themes. As a third-party organization, you should be wary about introducing new themes into an election unless you have the resources to ensure that voters can hear the message repeatedly. For example, if you choose to do direct mail and cannot do at least three separate mailings, your message will likely not be heard enough times to make an impact. Instead, build upon what your candidate is already talking about in their campaign. Look at their website and campaign literature to find the themes.

2. Focus your message on the issues that are most likely to win

Often times, issue-based political organizations stumble over the fact that they want to talk about their own cause. Certainly, if your cause is an issue that moves voters, you should recognize that. However, that isn't always the case. Voters may be more motivated by other key issues of the day. Issue-based organizations should not shy away from using unrelated issues to promote a candidate. If you are an environmental group, you should be willing to talk about health care. If you are a business group, you should be willing to talk about agriculture. The goal is for your candidate to win. If voters want to hear about a candidate's position on tax policy or better roads, then you need to make sure they hear about it. One of the reasons that polling is heavily encouraged when you are constructing your campaign plan is that it will help you identify the key issues that voters care about. Those can often be substantially different than the key issues you and your organization care about.

3. Rely on polling to link specific messages with the voters that will most likely be impacted by those messages

When you do have enough resources to repeat your own message in a campaign, then you more than likely also have the resources necessary to conduct polling. If you have good research (Chapter 12) and ask good questions (Chapter 13), then the polling will tell you which voters still have not made up their mind and what those undecided voters care about. Here are some important questions to consider when deciding what voters to target and with what messages:

→ Has the candidate locked down support from voters from their own party?
→ Are people from a certain section of the district largely undecided?
→ Do all voters care about the same issues, or does it vary by demographic (e.g., Do only men over the age of 65 care about lower taxes? Do women care more about education than health care?)?

It is a good exercise to write out the key groups of undecided voters and list the two or three issues each group cares about most. Then make sure to directly speak to the key undecided subgroups about how your candidate will address their concerns in your communications.

If you do not have polling, your best bet is to fall back on the official themes of your candidate's campaign. You can still choose to focus on specific groups of people you think the candidate needs to do better with, but that will be a judgment call based on anecdotal and historical experience. Some third-party groups choose to focus on traditional "swing" voters, which are usually defined as infrequent voters from both parties and independents.

Using these three guiding principles will help you identify the right message and the right voters to target. That is a huge step toward doing independent expenditures well. However, good campaign materials require more than the right message. In the next chapter we will discuss the best ways of getting this message out to voters.

TIP

Find ways to insert your issue into the election

We often hear from people who are disappointed that candidates are not talking more about their particular issue in an election. If this bothers you, there are things you can do to generate more attention, including:

- → Releasing news and reports during election season that causes the media and voters to pay more attention to a certain issue.
- → Organizing public events focused on your issues.
- → Coaching your supporters to ask questions of candidates about your issue at public forums.

However, you also need a dose of realism. Candidates are, as the old saying goes, "in it to win it." Through personal beliefs, public polling or anecdotal feedback, candidates have honed their campaign themes around issues that they believe voters care about. No matter how hard you may try, your issue may not be the one the electorate cares about in a particular year. You can still ensure candidates address it, but that may look different than a front page headline or a series of questions in a televised debate. Adjust your expectations. Demonstrate to candidates that there are smaller groups of important voters that do believe your issue is a priority. Arrange opportunities for candidates to meet these supporters. While it may not get the headlines you want, candidates will still be put in a position to address it and think about it.

CHAPTER 18

Contacting voters

Good campaign materials require strong execution as much as they require the right message.

Previously, you learned the importance of repetition, being flexible with your campaign messages, and choosing which voters you are going to speak to. Once you have the messages identified that will influence voters, you then need to consider two more factors that affect the effectivness of content: the medium and the delivery.

Choosing the right medium

The most challenging part of delivering a message through an independent expenditure has to do with figuring out what the candidate you support is already doing on their own. With independent expenditures you cannot be told what a candidate is planning by them or people working closely with their campaign. You are strictly limited by your best guess, what you see reported in their campaign finance reports and any materials they put out publicly.

Your goal is to fill in where the candidate is lacking, both in the type of voter contact and the people they are targeting. If you see or hear that a candidate is already sending half a dozen pieces of mail with targeted messaging for seniors, then focusing on that would not be a good use of your money. You can focus instead on the messages that persuade younger voters.

Additionally, you have to choose the right medium for the right audience. While you will reach some senior voters online, most are listening to a particular radio station or watching daytime, over-the-air television. Younger voters are on their phones and tend to use streaming services and social media.

You cannot be wedded to one medium of campaigning—be it radio, mail or canvassing. You have to be flexible in order to identify the right method to cover the platform the candidate is missing and use the platform that works for the voters you want to speak to.

Getting the delivery right

Delivery is what your voter contact looks and sounds like. Vendors will normally help you do this well (something we'll cover in the next chapter), but far too many candidates and political organizations try to cram a ton of words or complexity in a small space.

The reality is that very few voters read an entire piece of campaign literature. The most important parts of visual ads are good images and strong headlines. As many direct mail vendors will tell you, the time you have for your direct mail to influence a voter is the time it takes for them to walk from their mailbox to the trash can. Think about yourself. You are more than likely an above-average voter who has a greater interest in politics than your neighbors, and even you likely skim ads only very briefly.

That means for all types of visual ads you want things that are more graphically appealing to catch the eye and direct readers to the most important themes. You should have corroborating text on the piece that goes into further detail, as some voters will want to dive deeper and actually read what you sent them, but that should be the secondary priority for your content. Focus primarily on the first things that voters see: pictures and headlines.

Audio-based election content is not much different. When you create a radio ad or phone script, you want to focus on broad themes. Do not get into the weeds because you will lose your listener. Your voiceover should speak clearly, slowly and in short sentences. You can always provide more detailed content on your website for voters who want to dig deeper.

Negative campaigning is in the eye of the beholder

You haven't followed politics for long if you haven't heard someone rant about how much they dislike negative campaigning, or what most political operatives refer to as "contrast." However, the definition of negative campaigning usually depends on which side of the ad you sit on. Elections are about choices—Candidate A or Candidate B. That choice is often as much about what you don't like about Candidate B as much as it's about what you do like about Candidate A. This was true in the earliest political races in our Republic and it is true today. Even candidacies which are defined by hopeful, optimistic messaging spend a great deal of resources researching and contrasting themselves with their opponents.

This is a good thing. In a democratic system that is founded on the idea of informed voters, it is reasonable that voters should know about all relevant information that shows how elected officials may act if elected to public office. You should feel confident in communicating true and relevant information about candidates to voters. Where the line gets crossed is when organizations lie, mislead or bring up personal issues of no relevance to a candidate's qualifications. Do your best to scrutinize your content each and every time you do something that could be coined as "negative," and make sure you are not crossing that line.

You will often hear that "negative campaigning" will hurt the candidate doing it. As a general rule that is not true. There is a reason that nearly every candidate or third-party organization will engage in it. Voters respond to information they see as relevant. When it does backfire, it is when a candidate or third-party organization introduces an issue that voters find unbelievable or inappropriate. That simply means you need to be extra careful when selecting "contrast" messages, but you should not necessarily avoid contrast altogether.

CHAPTER 19

Hiring vendors

You need quality materials if you want to have a quality impact.

In most cases, people operating political organizations are best served by hiring a vendor to produce the independent expenditure materials that will be sent to voters. Political vendors have professional artists that make sure your materials catch the eye. They have writers who have experience working on hundreds of different campaigns.

In addition, you will be quite busy during an election with any number of other priorities on your plate. A vendor takes on the time-consuming work of production and distribution so that all you need to do is review content and provide edits.

There are some political organizations that produce their own independent expenditure content. However, that is an option that should be put off until you gain more experience.

Here are the most important things to keep in mind when hiring a vendor:

→ Most vendors specialize in one content area, such as media or print.
→ Most vendors are partisan. They will do work for candidates of one party. If your group is non-partisan, you may need to identify vendors from both sides of the aisle.
→ Look for vendors who know the local landscape very well. If your best option does not have local experience, scrutinize their production closely in case they choose images or text that are out of place or do not connect with the local audience.
→ Social and online advertising are still relatively new. Many vendors will claim to do this well. When interviewing them, ask how they will ensure the online ads are effective, rather than simply focusing on the number of views.
→ Just because you have a vendor does not mean you sign over all political decision-making to them. You are still the boss and should not feel pushed by a vendor to use issues or tactics that you do not think will work or are wrong.

While selecting a good vendor is important, they are only one group of people who can help you. Another key group are political allies who share a common interest in the election. We talk about building that political coalition in the next chapter.

There are easy ways to acquire a list of voters

If you are going to communicate directly with voters, the most basic information you need is a voter list. Lists are available to you at state or local election agencies. What is on the list will vary by jurisdiction, but the most consistent fields are name, age, political party, address, election districts and voting history. Each of those pieces of information helps you narrow down your list to the voters you want to speak to.

You may also acquire lists from vendors. The benefits of using a vendor is that they have done the grunt work of acquiring the information, and they often deliver it in a more user-friendly format. They are also more likely to have experience ensuring the information is accurate. There are companies easily found online that do this for anyone willing to pay the fee. Usually it is affordable. Sometimes the vendors you hire to do online ads, polling or direct mail will also acquire a voter list for you at a nominal additional cost.

There are vendors who specialize in voter data. They may cost more, but they can be more helpful in developing the strategy for specific voters and compiling a list of specific contact information for those voters. They may have good information about the best way to reach those voters, as well. Many list vendors do their own public polling to create models that predict what a voter may think about a particular message or issue based on what polling says about demographically similar individuals. It involves a lot of jargon and methods that can be intimidating to a political newcomer. It is worth pursuing though if you plan to spend a lot of resources on independent expenditures.

As you work with vendors, encourage them to stay out of the weeds and speak clearly about cost and exactly what they can deliver for you.

CHAPTER 20

Building political advocacy coalitions

When engaging in elections, do not go it alone if you do not have to.

Just as you want to do your best not to duplicate the efforts of the candidates in your independent expenditures, you also want to avoid duplicating the work of potential partners. There are any number of other issue groups doing the same thing you are in identifying and supporting candidates. Working with them could save you money and increase your odds of success. The way to do this effectively is to form political advocacy coalitions using these three steps.

Step 1: Identify the organizations that do direct election engagement

Look through candidate campaign finance reports and see which organizations show up repeatedly. Ask candidates if other groups are speaking with them. In most states there are political organizations associated with realtors, builders, labor, social causes, business, education, the environment, etc. You may want to search for politically active groups associated with certain sectors.

Step 2: Find common alignment

Identify organizations that are supporting your top candidates and approach them about working together. Because elected officials are diverse people, you may find, on occasion, your allies prefer a different candidate. It is rare for you to have perfect alignment with another organization, particularly when you work on different causes. Use this opportunity to discuss why you disagree. Perhaps you can prevail on them to change their mind or remain neutral. In the end, if you find that you are supporting a different candidate than a partner do not be dismayed. Eventually this happens to everyone in coalition politics. Make sure the organizations you work with are prepared to handle these situations professionally and just "agree to disagree."

Political parties are a distinct possibility for an alliance, although some states consider political parties an extension of the candidates. In this case, you have to be aware of coordination laws. Political parties are always looking for organizations that can help their candidates. However, they are also the organizations most likely to expect total allegiance. For ideological or strategic reasons, they may not be comfortable working closely with non-partisan organizations.

Step 3: Put the relationships to work

Once you have built your network of political allies, there are many ways to help each other:

→ Share intelligence about likely candidates.
→ Share what you are hearing from candidates about each other's issues.
→ Work together to recruit candidates.
→ If allowed by law, coordinate independent expenditures so you do not duplicate activities.

Seeking non-traditional allies is an effective strategy when working to pass new laws during the legislative process, as well. We will discuss this more in Chapter 25. However, before we can get to the work of passing laws, we have to deal with the results of the election. In the next section, we discuss important steps to ensure you maximize your impact after an election is over.

Post-election to-dos

Section 4

IN THIS SECTION

CHAPTER 21

Ensuring your election work is noticed

Your work is not finished on Election Night because a complete plan includes follow-up.

The election is over, but don't pack your bags for a post-election vacation yet! Political advocates often forget one of the most critical components: talking about the election once it is done.

Because you are living it every day, you tend to think that everyone is fully aware of everything you did in the election. The reality is that few people fully comprehend the scope of your involvement, including candidates, political leaders, media and your own supporters. In this section we will talk about how to talk about your election work after it is over, including specific instructions for key groups you should address.

It is important to provide a recap because you are trying to build a reputation. Moving forward, you want elected officials who are friends of your cause to know that you will stand with them when they need you most. Knowing the extent of your involvement encourages and emboldens them. You want your supporters to understand how their donations were spent and to know what comes next.

There are a few general guidelines you should follow for effective post-election reporting:

- **Evaluate your results.** Before you do any public reporting, you need to assess what occurred so you can craft the right narrative. A public report of your election activity needs to be more than a list. It needs to tell a story. You likely had an expectation coming into the election on what would signify great progress, good progress or a poor result. Before sharing your results with others, honestly evaluate your results against the goals you set. Did you need to grow your support in order to advance your cause? Did you need to protect some key allies in order to maintain your momentum? Did you expect to take a step back, but were able to limit losses?
- **Be humble and realistic.** There is a fine line in politics between not taking enough credit and taking too much. When you recap elections, remember that you engaged as a third-party organization. The most important piece of the puzzle was the candidate. Never appear to take more credit for a win than the candidate. Use words like "helped" and "assisted."
- **Do it quickly.** Political observers move quickly after an election to draw conclusions. Your allies are starving for information. If you want to be relevant, you not only need to report what you did but you need to do it as soon as possible. Media should hear from you by the evening of the election or the first thing in the morning. Your supporters should get a brief update from you on Election Night or by the day after, followed by a more comprehensive update within a week.

These are general parameters that will serve you well with any post-election report. However, when it comes to giving the right report to the right people, there are important specifics to consider. We tackle post-election reporting in more detail in the next chapter when we walk through tips on communicating with specific groups of people.

CHAPTER 22

Distributing post-election reports

As with any effective message, it is important to say the right thing to the right people in your post-election reports.

By now, you have seen that in politics you often deliver different messages and information to different groups of people. Following an election, you have sensitive information that is not appropriate for everyone. There are different messages, levels of detail and types of sensitive information that you provide to candidates, political leaders, media and your supporters, and your communication to each group serves a specific purpose, shaping how each group reacts to your political efforts.

Candidates

For the candidates you supported, your goal is to ensure they know what you did on their behalf.

You should reach out to them after the election in two ways. If you did independent expenditures, create a short memo detailing all you did and include samples of voter contact, such as mail or radio ads, if you have them available. You can mail the information or, ideally, set up an appointment to meet them in person. If they won, this is also a good opportunity to talk about the ways you can help them navigate policymaking in their newly elected position.

Secondly, following the election, write form letters to send to all candidates you endorsed. Create one version for those who were not successful and another version for those who were successful and mail the letters within a week of the election. Tell them you recognized their hard work. If they won, express how happy you are for them. If they lost, congratulate them on a hard-fought race and encourage them to stay involved. Perhaps they are someone you can plug into your own advocacy efforts moving forward. Many candidates who lost still have strong local networks and are recognized community leaders.

Political Leaders

This group includes legislative leaders, key elected officials who work with you, key allies from other causes, and, in some cases, the media. Your goal in speaking to them is to build a reputation as an organization that will have a strong, ongoing presence in the political system.

This requires a more detailed memo that has a longer analysis of your election work. Some tips:

- → Stay positive as a general rule.
- → Spend a page or two explaining your impact in elections and how it has furthered your cause.
- → Feature a handful of races you engaged in that were the most significant wins.
- → For each candidate you supported in a significant way, write one or two paragraphs explaining your efforts. It is safe to include dollar figures in post-election reports because all of those expenditures should have been publicly reported. If, for reasons specific to your state, you did not have to publicly report dollars spent in support of a candidate, then you will have to determine whether you want people to know that information.

No matter how limited your distribution of this document is, never assume that anything you put in a memo like this will remain confidential. Write it assuming it will have wide distribution.

Key Supporters, Donors and Board Members

For the purpose of this chapter, a supporter is any person with whom you are comfortable sharing sensitive information. This might include donors and board members. The goal for this group is to thank them, analyze what worked and what did not work, and leave them feeling encouraged about the fight ahead.

This is a memo that is an expanded version of what you send to political leaders, but where you dive into more detail, including a comprehensive, realistic assessment of what occurred in the election. While this document is internal, you should always be aware that something put in writing could be distributed more widely than you intended.

Many of the people reading this memo are not going to have the time or the desire to read many detailed pages, so keep that in mind. However, you do want to list election results for all the candidates you supported. Present a detailed breakdown of the election spending. Even your supporters may not have kept all the races straight, so include information about geographic location of the candidates.

Distribute the memo via email or, if feasible, schedule face-to-face meetings with supporters to present the report in person.

Media

Your goal in speaking to the media is to ensure your organization is featured in their recap of the election and you are referenced in the post-election narrative as an organization that made a significant difference.

A bigger question, however, is whether you should proactively communicate with the media after an election. It is not as essential as you might think. If you do your post-election communications correctly, your key audiences will hear from you directly. A proactive media presence becomes more important when you believe your issue will be or should be part of their post-election articles. Focus your press release on the political race or races that the media cares the most about.

Get your recap to the media as quickly as possible after an election concludes. That means you may want to draft a press release in advance based on several likely scenarios and fill in the blanks after the election concludes.

Distribute your press release to political reporters at major publications and stations in your area or state. Do not get into the weeds. Summarize your involvement briefly, provide your perspective about the election results, and include a brief quote from your primary spokesperson.

Also consider sending your press release to local, politically-focused blogs and newsletters. They often do post-election recaps and it can be good for your reputation to have a third-party validator reference your activity. Given that their readership is interested in politics, consider sharing a more lengthy recap similar to what you share with political leaders.

CHAPTER 23

Handling lost elections

If you engage in politics, you are bound to have some bad elections, and that's okay.

Most people choose not to engage in electoral politics because they are afraid of losing. They believe that losing will set back the issues they care about. They are afraid of rejection. That fear is part of our nature but we have to push passed it if we are going to better serve our cause.

Sometimes when you engage in elections, your candidates win. However, if you engage in politics long enough, you will have bad election nights. Your cause may seem defeated with no glimmer of hope for the future. After the 2016 election, one in which the two primary candidates for president had an extremely close election, decided by the narrowest of margins, the media seemed ready to declare the losing party adrift. Yet, two years later, fortunes had been reversed. Politics is cyclical.

So, yes, there will be times when you will be rejected. If you choose to engage in politics, rejection is simply part of the process. You will survive if you react positively and with renewed fervor, knowing your time will come. Most prominent politicians have lost an election. Famously, Abraham Lincoln lost his race for U.S. Senate before going on two years later to win the presidency. There is only one guarantee in politics: if you do not engage in elections, you will lose a key chance to advance your cause. Assuming you conduct yourself professionally and ethically, and you do not give up, you will survive a bad election.

The funny thing about elections is that you can also derive victories from losses. Here are some examples:

→ Elected officials do not like close elections. After close elections, you might find elected officials you opposed more open to discussion in the hopes of finding ways to work together in the future. Other elected officials that were not up for election may have noticed, too. They may want to avoid the same political headache when they face reelection.

→ Your work may embolden future candidates who know there is an organization that will stand by them. You will learn valuable lessons that will guide you in the next election.

→ You may have been able to engage your grassroots supporters in the election activity. Even in a loss, you will likely walk away with a more motivated grassroots army.

Of course, we do not want to lose. Certainly, a loss requires a close evaluation of your strategies and tactics. After a loss you will want to be candid and transparent with your supporters. You should promise and deliver a comprehensive analysis of the election and the factors that led to the losses. However, strive to avoid the tendency to think the sky is falling. Provide a few simple, realistic goals for getting your efforts back on track. Always remind your supporters of the importance of what you are fighting for. Find the positives, learn from the mistakes and move on to the next political fight.

Lobbying for lasting change

Section 5

IN THIS SECTION

CHAPTER 24

Choosing a lobbyist

Lobbyists can help open doors and make your case, but you should look before you leap into the world of lobbying.

Political advocacy is about more than just elections. The most effective advocates have learned the hard way that even when you have the best representatives, if they don't hear from you and your supporters before, during and after the legislative session, your cause will suffer. That is why lobbying is so important.

One way to ensure you are lobbying effectively is to hire a professional. Before choosing a lobbyist, you should first think through whether you actually need one to achieve your long-term goals. Also, be aware that if you lobby or hire a lobbyist, it may trigger additional registration and reporting with your state or locality.

What kinds of entities would hire a lobbyist and why?

→ Organizations, causes or businesses may hire a lobbyist if they do not have a full-time employee dedicated to being present where elected officials are meeting.
→ Organizations with a full-time staff person who lobbies may want additional lobbying support if their staff person cannot meet with elected officials often enough or the bill they are working requires them to speak to more officials than they can reasonably handle. A lobbyist can help fill those gaps and ensure the organization is consistently updated on happenings.
→ Organizations that want someone with a better knowledge of important people or processes that would help pass the bill.

If you decide to hire a lobbyist, be careful about allowing them to be the face of your issue or organization. The position of a lobbyist is often temporary and they represent a myriad of issues. Relationships with elected officials are valuable. Your first priority should be to build them yourself and to use the resources within your organization.

Even with a good lobbyist, your success still comes down to whether you have good legislation and good arguments. You also have to stay on top of managing a lobbyist. They have multiple interests. They may not push an elected official as hard because they have to maintain relationships for all their clients.

Additionally, lobbyists are expensive. Lobbyists often require yearlong contracts or they pack large retainers into the short time period of session. You can negotiate. Be confident coming into the conversation by knowing what you are willing to pay. In most cases, you are best served when you stick to that amount.

After scrutiny, you may decide hiring a lobbyist is worthwhile. Here are basic questions to consider when hiring a lobbyist:

→ Do they have a good reputation?
→ Can you afford them?
→ Will they work hard for you?
→ Do they believe in what you are doing?

Lobbyists perform an important service for organizations like yours, but do not feel like you have no choice. Your funds are limited. Do not sign on the dotted line without asking yourself the tough questions first.

CHAPTER 25

Building coalitions for legislative success

When seeking allies to help you advance your cause, don't limit yourself to the obvious.

We previously discussed working with coalitions in the context of political campaigns. In this chapter, we expore how to work with coalitions to advance your legislative goals.

In politics, it is often the case that overcoming the differences with your friends is more difficult than overcoming the differences with your foes. There are turf battles, hidden agendas and lack of coordination. One of the worst situations is when elected officials get mixed messages from organizations that they presume should be working together. Despite these soap opera-worthy storylines, building coalitions really is one of the most vital parts of being successful.

Legislative coalitions can be hard because people are complex. You may be competing for funding with your friends or you have a different take on legislative strategies, which is understandable. Here are a few tips for working better with your allies:

→ **Build relationships.** Spending more social time with your allies can help to soften the hard edges. Personal relationships build trust and can help you better evaluate and understand the motives of other people. Consider regular dinners or social outings with legislative allies.

→ **Develop patience for different types of people.** This is not always so easy, but make a conscious effort not to let the lack of a personal connection affect the way you view someone professionally. There will undoubtedly be people you will not "click" with, but that shouldn't mean you can't work together.

- → **Focus less on who should get the credit.** This is a major hurdle in legislative coalitions. While there is some need to self-promote, your primary goal is getting the job done. Focus on where you can offer added value rather than focusing on how to get your name in the headlines. Set an example in the coalition by remembering to thank and include everyone. If you work hard and well, you will be recognized for your role.
- → **Don't just talk about coordination.** Coalition meetings are often overly long, with lots of talking and little action. Encourage your coalition to have specific objectives and outcomes for meetings. Think critically about where each organization has a role, and be self-aware enough to know when something is not your specialty.
- → **Err on the side of over-communication.** Many coalition problems occur not because other allies don't like what you are doing, but because you did not tell anyone about it beforehand. A 10-minute phone call once or twice a week just to check in with allies and keep them apprised of your work will do wonders.

Finally, it is easy to know which groups share your exact same policy priorities. However, effective coalition building involves looking beyond the obvious and thinking of organizations that have a *tangential* interest in your issue. Examples would include pre-school education advocates allying with businesses who are interested in a more prepared workforce. A coalition could include farm groups and business organizations that share a similar interest in tax reform. Or perhaps a coalition could bring together an environmental conservation group and a labor organization whose members care about environmental issues because of the environmental dangers they deal with at work.

Your unconventional allies may not be intimately involved with your plan every step of the way, but they could help at key moments, such as introducing you to a key legislator they know or building your credibility by publicly supporting your cause.

CHAPTER 26

Deciding on the best ways to contact an elected official

Elected officials will tell you they do not like to be harassed, but you need to create a drumbeat of constant communications.

Elected officials may twist you into knots with their advice to you about how to communicate with them. On a piece of tough legislation, they may ask you to generate examples of constituents that support it. Unfortunately, that is often a sign that they are looking for an excuse to vote no and they may not side with you even if you meet their demand. Other times when you flood their inbox or phone line, they will get upset and tell you to stop or that they don't care for form letters. Ironically, in both cases the reality may be the opposite of what they are telling you.

How do you wade through those mixed messages? The simple answer is that constituent contacts with elected officials are almost always helpful to your cause as long as the people contacting the elected officials are being civil and fair. It is also important that they live within the elected official's district. It is undoubtedly more effective when constituents send personalized emails or make phone calls without having to be coached. Any time you can generate a more organic response, you should. Look for advocacy technology that prompts constituents to create more personalized interactions, but do not underestimate the value of voter contacts even if it is a form letter. As much as the elected official kicks and screams, they know that letter came from a voter and they know that the voter had to take personal time to send it, form letter or not.

Here are five things to remember when encouraging constituent contacts:

- → Supporters should contact their own elected officials.
- → Phone calls are a more personal touch, but they are harder to get grassroots supporters to complete and supporters may struggle to explain their position on the phone.
- → When asking constituents to send emails, draft one or more sample messages and ask people to copy and paste them into an email. Or you can use a voter-contact software platform that pre-loads a suggested email but then allows people to edit it if they choose.
- → Keep all phone calls, letters and emails short. Ask your supporters to quickly state their position at the beginning and include only two or three brief points in support.
- → Keep the messages direct and positive.

If you want to improve the impact of these email and phone blitzes, consider organizing person-to-person interactions to validate the constituent contacts the elected official is receiving via phone and email. Bring small groups of constituents to an elected official for a meeting. Organize a house party and invite the elected official. It often does not take many voters to get an elected official's attention.

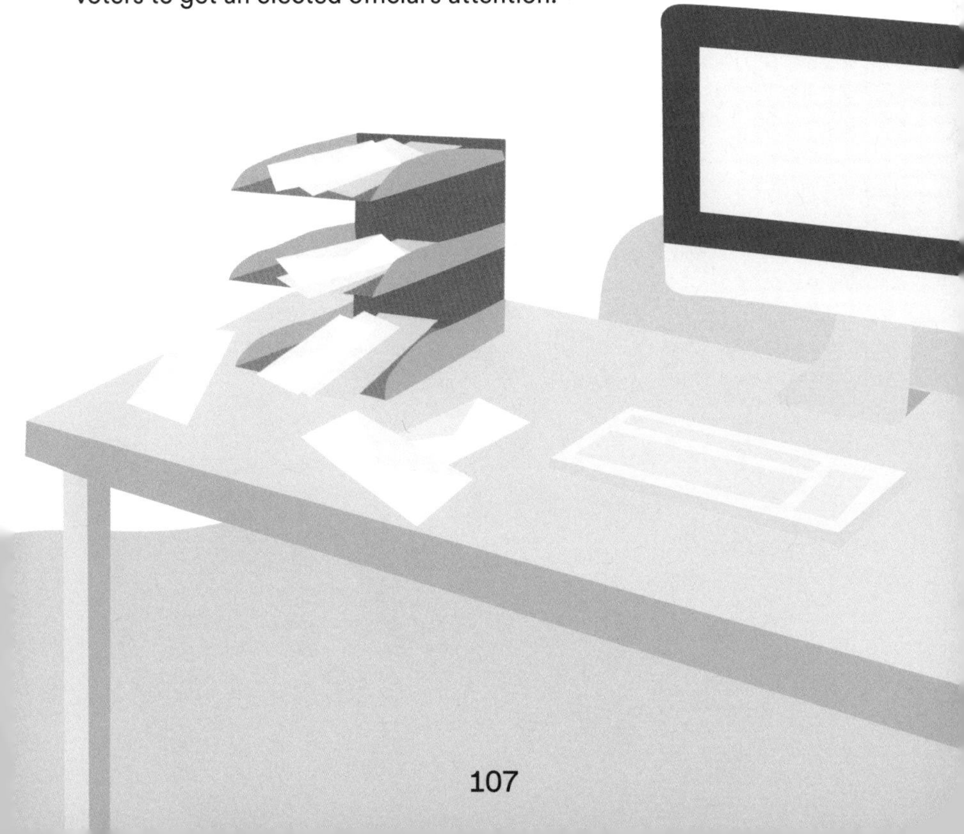

CHAPTER 27

Preparing for a meeting with an elected official

There is nothing more fundamental to advocacy than taking your issue directly to an elected official.

While all tactics related to lobbying are important, the most basic form of lobbying is simply sitting down with an elected official and making your case. Ideally, you hope a simple conversation is all it will take to persuade an elected official to side with you. It does not always work out that way, but it is the one lobbying tactic that you must try. You may choose to skip letters-to-the-editor or fancy television ads, but you can't avoid the step of actually talking to an elected official.

If you are in a one-on-one meeting you must be prepared. This is your best opportunity to persuade an elected official and you will make an important first impression about your legislation.

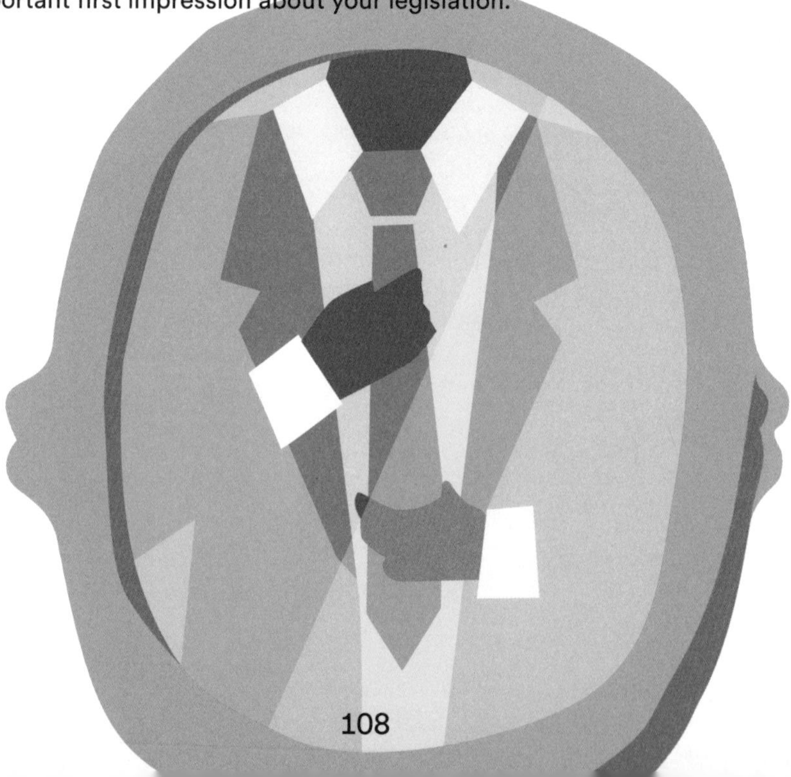

Use these tips to prepare for an in-person meeting:

→ **Sketch out the two or three key points you want to get across in the meeting.** Resist the urge to get into the weeds unless the elected official requests it. They have many different issues they are tracking. Focus on the arguments you believe will be most effective and memorable for that particular elected official.
→ **Do your research.** Do you have indications or past history that tells you what this elected official cares about or thinks in regards to your issue?
→ **Bringing multiple people to a meeting is okay and often good.** One person may remember a fact or argument that another person may not. Another person may have a unique experience to share. However, be careful about overwhelming an elected official by bringing too large of a group to a meeting. Generally, you should limit attendees to two or three. A large group may cause an elected official to be guarded and defensive. There are unique instances where stakes are high and you want an elected official to feel uncomfortable, but do not make this your default. And definitely do not bring a large group without the elected official knowing it ahead of time.
→ **Paper helps.** Have a brief document to leave with the elected official after the meeting that reiterates your points and provides supporting material for each point.
→ **Be on time and be flexible if they are delayed.** Understand that an elected official's schedule can change suddenly. Their time is often limited, too. Keep your primary remarks brief and to the point to ensure the meeting does not end before you have finished. If there is additional time, you can be prepared to ask the elected official questions or have some secondary arguments to present.
→ **Leave room for feedback.** End the conversation by asking the elected official if there is any additional information you could provide about the issue that would be helpful. Not only are you offering to be of service, but their answer often reveals parts of your issue that they are struggling with.

In the next chapter we move beyond one-one-one discussions and discuss interactions with full committees where elected officials hear public testimony about an issue.

CHAPTER 28

Giving effective testimony before elected officials

This can be the part of advocacy that advocates fear the most, but good preparation can calm the nerves.

Nearly every bill is required to be discussed in a public hearing before elected officials may vote on it. This gives you an opportunity as an advocate to make your case in front of other constituents, the media and elected officials.

Public speaking is hard and intimidating for most people. It is perfectly normal to feel this way. Despite the elevated desks and glaring eyes, it is important to remember that elected officials are people too. They likely felt the same way you did before they were elected and speaking publicly became more routine for them with practice.

Here are a few tips to get you through the experience:

- **Bring notes.** Do not hesitate to write out your remarks and read them if you think you will struggle in your delivery.
- **Pay close attention to what others are saying during testimony.** While it is OK to touch on something others have covered, if someone who speaks before you did a good job laying out a point you should avoid completely rehashing it.
- **Be respectful of time.** Not only will you be unlikely to keep their attention with a lengthy speech, but the hearings can get very long. Keep your remarks brief.
- **Speak slowly.** You should almost always speak more slowly than you think you need to and enunciate clearly.
- **Do not hesitate to disagree with an elected official, but be civil and respectful.** Do not put words in their mouth or accuse them of insidious motives. This is not only a bad look, but it often backfires. Most of the people you disagree with have pure motives and you both ultimately want the same goal. Your path of getting there is just different.

Build better relationships with elected officials by first focusing on how you can help them

It does not always seem like it, but most elected officials enter public office a little intimidated. They are being asked to master issues they have never heard of. They are usually part time and have little or no staff. Many people are suddenly putting a lot of pressure on these officials to make difficult decisions. So elected officials are often looking for a few friends.

It is a bad habit of advocacy organizations to only see elected officials when they want something, such as a vote on a tough policy question. This does not mean you should not have those conversations. However, you will be in a much better position to have those conversations if you have laid the groundwork to let a lawmaker know you are there to help make their life easier, too.

To begin with, strive to meet with as many elected officials as possible during downtime. Visit them in their local districts. Seek to understand their personal priorities and background.

Secondly, offer to do background research for them when you have expertise on a topic they want to learn more about. You want elected officials to know they can rely on you.

Lastly, as long as there is some tangential relationship to your own cause, consider helping an elected official on another policy priority. Most will remember and appreciate it.

Advising people to "put others first" is not new. But this ancient tip for building better relationships holds true today as much as it did thousands of years ago.

CHAPTER 29

Playing offense and defense in legislative advocacy

It is important to be aggressive in policy advocacy, even when it feels like you are on your heels.

Advocacy is not always about creating new laws. Sometimes it is about defending the good laws we already have or stopping bad ideas. However, it can be tiring to constantly be playing defense. In sports, it is well known that a team which is always on the defensive will tire more quickly than the offensive team. So to steal an adage common to athletics, it's helpful for advocates to adopt the mindset that "the best defense is a good offense."

If you do legislative advocacy for a long time, you have to understand that you will inevitably have peaks and valleys. Issues become more or less trendy. Certain political philosophies rise and fall. The media will declare one political party "dead" after an awful election night only to flip the script two years later. A powerful elected official will be leading the political body one year and then will lose in a primary election the next year. Getting upset by these things is like a sailor getting upset about the tide.

While advocates can't change the cyclical nature of politics, the best advocates do take advantage of it in two ways:

→ **When they have momentum, they take full advantage of it.** Push fast and push hard. Take as much ground as you can when you are playing offense. While you may have multiple years of success, do not assume it will last forever. Remind your allies of this, particularly the elected officials who often become fixated on self-preservation and hesitate to take the chances necessary to have an impact.

→ **They don't let a reversal of fortune get them down.** You need to prepare yourself, your team and your supporters for downturns. Cultivate donors who will help see you through these lulls. Coach your team to understand political cycles. Finally, look forward to the challenge and opportunity of playing defense in order to protect the hard-fought wins you achieved during the good times.

When the political winds shift, and it is your turn to play defense, it is important to remember that playing defense creates opportunities for your organization. For one, defense is easier. Never assume your opponents have the upper hand. It is very hard to pass a law. Just like the "no" vote on an initiative or referendum is easier to win, it is human nature to be suspicious of something new. Jump in with energy because you could succeed in holding back your opponents.

Second, playing defense gives your organization a platform to rally your supporters. While you may often wonder where your allies were when you were trying to pass your own legislation, adversity has a way of bringing people out. Take advantage of this by restocking your grassroots advocacy forces. Be public and vocal. Your resistance may be noticed by funders who are looking for bold leaders.

Last, you never know when a win may be possible. Even when fighting an attempt by your opponents to end policies that you support, it is important to "play offense" with positive legislation you would like to see enacted. This communicates to elected officials that they cannot get rid of you easily. It helps steer debate. It provides opportunities to compromise in ways that work in your favor. Additionally, politics is highly unpredictable. There are circumstances wholly out of your control that can create unexpected momentum for your policy ideas. Due to an emerging crisis or a well-placed elected ally, a brief window of opportunity may open. If you have no positive legislation crafted and introduced, you may lose the chance.

If you look at defense as an opportunity to retrench and rebuild, you may get some unexpected wins and a stronger organization for your next peak.

In our final chapter we will discuss one of the biggest errors advocates make when pushing for change: they often forget to say thank you.

CHAPTER 30

Remembering to say thank you

It is true that we catch more flies with honey, but we often neglect this easy and important piece of the puzzle.

Being an elected official is often a thankless job. It can feel like a never-ending chain of attacks. Think about your own life. Are you more likely to concede in an argument when you are berated? Quite the opposite. You grow defensive and dig in your heels.

We often forget the power of a kind word. Even when meeting with an elected official to talk about an issue where you are in disagreement, take a moment to thank them. Thank them for a recent action they took. Thank them for attending an important meeting. Thank them for their service.

If it is warranted and legally allowed, consider presenting elected officials who distinguish themselves in their support of your cause with a recognition or award. Make it an organizational habit to do this every year for your favorite elected officials. Present them with a certificate, promote their service on your social media channels, or honor them at an event. The latter is a great way to show public appreciation and bring together your supporters for yet another opportunity to interact with elected officials and to show off your broad grassroots support.

It is also nice to take your "thanks" public. Let the citizens of the elected official's district know the official was a phenomenal leader for your issue through direct mail, radio, online or earned media. Many of the issues we discussed in the section on creating independent expenditures apply here as well—stick to broad themes and good design, and check laws to see if any of these activities are restricted. Legislators generally love this attention as it helps them have more productive conversations with voters.

Taking tough stands in politics can wear out elected officials. They are facing more criticism than ever before. Make sure they know you appreciate their work.

The 50CAN community

Conclusion

IN THIS SECTION

If we've reached our goals with this book, by now you are feeling a bit more prepared to engage in the political process to advance your cause. Now comes the fun part: getting down to work! That's where we come in. 50CAN was created to provide a home base and a supportive community for advocates like you. We aim to be a place where talented people are able to do the best work of their lives in a culture that supports and sustains them. The glue that holds this community together is a team spirit grounded in our shared commitment to putting our cause at the center of our advocacy world.

Our P.O.R.C.H. values

What defines us as a community are the values we aim to uphold in our daily work.

Plussing it
Borrowing a phrase from Walt Disney, we challenge ourselves to do great work and then go a step beyond that...and then a step beyond that. We strive for "better" and "best" on behalf of our cause.

Optimism
We believe deeply in the American Dream and our ability to foster real change in our communities, even when faced with seemingly insurmountable odds. We approach tough challenges with high spirits.

Relentless
We are dogged in pursuit of our mission and our goals. We don't back down.

Candor
We are authentic about our challenges, mistakes and triumphs. We're honest with others and with ourselves.

Humility
We know we don't have all the answers and that we can only succeed by constantly testing our assumptions, working in deep collaboration with others and grounding ourselves in diverse viewpoints from across our states. We learn from our successes and our failures and strive to constantly improve.

Our work

At 50CAN, we want to learn from and contribute to the work of as many citizen advocates as possible. The cause at the center of our work is education. We support individuals at the local level who advocate for a high-quality education for all kids, regardless of their address. We've built a team that provides citizen advocates with trusted research and proven tools so they can drive the creation of stronger, more equitable schools in every state and community in our country.

How can you join our community of education advocates?

Continue your journey online
Want to learn more about some of the tactics we use? Need extra templates and worksheets for your campaigns? Visit guidebook.50can.org for these resources and more. Be sure to check back often. We'll be continuing to update the page with new tips and materials as our network grows.

Sign up for our emails
Want to learn more about what we are doing right now? Sign up for our emails at 50can.org so we can keep you plugged in to everything happening across our network.

Apply to a training program
We offer both full-time and part-time training programs and other opportunities for engagement across the country. Find out more about these programs and how to apply on the Programs page of our website.

Share your progress
Take a picture of your campaign plan and post it on social media using the hashtag #OpenAdvocacy. Then, text 50CAN to 52886 to sign up for our text action alerts!

Start the conversation
Sometimes the best place to start is with a conversation. We would love to hear from you and talk about how we might be able to work together. Email us at partnerships@50can.org and we will respond with a way to take the next step.

Join a campaign
We aren't in all 50 states yet, but if we are in your state, we would love for you to get involved as a volunteer, intern, staff member or advisory board member. Visit the Careers page on our website to find out more about opportunities within our current campaigns.

Sample election engagement timeline

The following is a sample timeline that gives you a sense of the standard order that you will follow when choosing to engage in elections. It includes a range of time that activities are usually conducted.

1. Assessing upcoming political climate and identifying your political goals

Summer previous year → December previous year
You should begin to pencil in an election strategy and identify opportunities for you to use the upcoming election cycle to improve the conditions for your issue. Plans can change but it is important to begin preparing yourself and your closest supporters.

2. Recruiting candidates

Summer previous year → filing deadline
It often takes a long time to find viable candidates and for them to consider filing. You want to give yourself ample time so that the candidates not only beat the filing deadline but have time to mount a full campaign.

3. Initial plan drafted

Fall previous year → December previous year
Have your initial plan drafted based on your best information available. This plan will be used to guide your candidate research and fundraising.

4. Candidate research

Fall previous year → 6 weeks prior to election
You can begin as soon as you have a strong idea that you will be supporting or opposing a candidate. Sooner the better if you want to utilize the information fully.

5. Candidate interviews

Fall previous year → 1 month prior to election
You can begin interviewing candidates as soon as they begin to officially announce their intentions.

6. Fundraising

Fall previous year → 1 month prior to election
Potential donors often take time to become comfortable with your strategies. Start early so they have time to think and become invested in the strategy. Additionally, it is quite hard to balance election engagement and fundraising simultaneously.

7. Release candidate questionnaire

4 months prior to election → 6 weeks prior to election
You need to release these soon enough to give candidates ample time to complete them and time for you to evaluate them before you have to make electoral support decisions. You may have to release it before the actual candidate filing deadline and continue to distribute it as candidates announce.

8. Election Polling

3 months prior to election → 3 weeks prior to election
Ideally, you are polling as close as possible to the time that your final electoral support decisions are made so you are acting on the latest and best information. Polling less than three weeks out from an election makes it dificult for most organizations to act on the information.

9. Final election engagement plan

3 months prior to election → 1 month prior to election
Understanding that there are always last minute twists and turns, you need your final plan set early enough so your electoral engagement has its maximum impact on voters.

10. Direct contribution distribution

3 months prior to election → 2 weeks prior to election
Theoretically, you can give donations to candidates whenever it is convenient, assuming there are not legal restrictions on it. Many elected officials have fundraising events a year or more out from their election. However, there is a time when it becomes too late. Candidates prefer you to make donations at least two or three months out from the election. It allows them to make better plans for their most intense period of spending in the run-up to the election. Donations less than a couple weeks before the election do not give candidates as much flexibility in using the funds.

11. Voter contact for independent expenditures (most intense period)

2 months prior to election → Election Day
While you may from time to time talk to voters earlier in the cycle, this is when you will spend the most time and money doing it. American voters are making voting decisions earlier and earlier. In many states, mail, absentee or in-person voting starts about one month before Election Day.

My notes

My notes

Printed and bound in the USA by SOURCEALL MEDIA